Broken
and
Spilled Out
(An Abuse Recovery Journal)
Recovering Yourself

K. J. Sharpe

Sharpe Turns Publishing; A division of Sharpe Turns LLC

Library of Congress Numbers: 002188171, 001671403

ISBN: 978-0-578-66854-3

Most scriptures from the King James Version and New King James Version from Bible Gateway, www.biblegateway.com operated by The Zondervan Corporation LLC. All Rights Reserved. Used by permission.
Other scriptures from the Holy Bible, New International Version®, ©1973, 1978, 1984, 2011 by Biblica, Inc. Used by permission. All rights reserved worldwide.

Disclaimer: All information contained herein is for educational, informational, and inspirational purposes. No guarantees of any kind are declared or implied as legal, financial, medical, or professional advice. A great deal of effort has been made to present information and resources as accurately and up to date as possible. The author/publisher is not liable, directly or indirectly for any loss or damage incurred as a result of the use of information contained in this document, including but not limited to errors, inaccuracies, or omissions. Please consult licensed professionals for any legal, medical, physical, or psychological needs, issues, or questions you may have.

Printed in the United States of America

DEDICATED TO MY MOTHER

Gloria Jean Daniels

"Who can find a virtuous woman? for her price is far above rubies."
-Proverbs 31:10 (KJV)

Special thanks to my mother, Gloria Jean Daniels, the virtuous woman. She is a priceless commodity, her value worth more than precious jewels. She is a mighty woman of valor, a warrior who holds back the enemies of the soul. From the cradle to the grave, hers is the hand that rocks, rules, and heals the world. She is student and teacher, mentor, master, and servant. She is the weaver of cloth as well as dreams, the spinner of magical love that forever holds, binds, and hopes. She is the catcher of tears and the reaper of joy. She is fortified with strength and endowed with weakness, both of which cause her to seek the face of an immortal, omniscient, and all-powerful God. She is toughness and tenderness, wisdom and faith, conqueror and constant in season and out of time. She is my shero. Loved and beloved, she is the woman who taught me, by example, how to weather every storm. I love you mom.

K. J. Sharpe

FOREWORD

I was a preacher's kid, PK for short. That's what they call you when you are the child of a minister. My father was a no-nonsense pastor. He was extremely strict both at home and when it came to church business.

At church, there were only two instruments allowed: a piano and an organ, no exceptions. My father was the boss and what he said had to be obeyed, no matter what. Everyone had to conform to his rules. Even his deacons, the men responsible for church matters, were afraid of him. It wasn't much different at home, especially if you were a child. I was unhappy and dissatisfied with many things as a child but in those days, children didn't have a voice. Even if you were called names like dumb, stupid, and told you would never amount to anything, you wouldn't dare talk back to your parents. Your only answer had better be yes ma'am, no ma'am, yes sir, or no sir. I learned well not to buck the system at church or at home.

My abuser was six feet tall and 250 pounds to my five feet one, 120 pounds. I had one child, a daughter. He threatened to kill my child, using those threats against me to make me do everything he said. I didn't know how to leave. I had no place to go. Then one day when I was at church my pastor said, "Someone in here has a spirit of fear on them. God did not give you a spirit of fear, but of power, and of love, and of a sound mind." I knew that was for me. I went to my pastor and his wife after service to talk to them about my situation. They not only told me to leave; they also invited me to come stay with them. This freed and empowered me. Despite my petite stature, I became a bold sister, ready to fight. I was even willing to die to protect my child.

Speaking out against domestic violence has since been one of my enduring passions. As CEO and President of D.C. Alliance Empowering

Homicide Survivors Inc., established in 2010, we have offered domestic violence training and community support in the form of advocacy, education, people connecting in trusted productive environments, anger management, personal growth and development, and chaplaincy services for families of homicide victims. We created the online *Interfaith Fellowship Services Praise Ministry*, spiritual enrichment programs for mental health, and offer counseling, supports, and supplies for homeless shelters. We created a youth *Library of Peace* at The Covenant House in Washington, D.C. In 2019 we were chosen by the D. C.'s Department of Corrections as *Volunteer of the Year* from over 300 churches. We were the only organization providing holy communion for inmates. We were the first to develop a National Domestic Violence Conference in Washington, D.C. Our work continues. I met K. J. Sharpe through this work.

As a pastor and spiritual pastoral care advisor, I share my personal story in workshops and trainings to give context to sexual abuse and domestic violence. Women in faith communities are often told that married couples are supposed to stay married even in cases of abuse because "God will take care of it." It is inexcusable that this abominable lie still resounds in churches today. According to Matthew 22:37-39 (NIV), Jesus said, "Love the Lord your God with all your heart and with all your soul and mind. This is the first and greatest commandment. And the second is like it: love your neighbor as yourself." Despite this truth, abuse victims are still condemned to silence, the stories of their devastated lives shoved under the covers without anyone being held accountable for the damage. The goal is control and, as a result, many members feel stuck, afraid, and ashamed, never disclosing their pain.

No one deserves to be abused mentally, physically, spiritually, sexually, emotionally, or otherwise. That's not love. Yet many religious communities reject any teaching, training, or make a sincere attempt at addressing the problem in a loving, productive, safe way. Hosea 4:6 (NIV) says, "My people are destroyed for lack of knowledge. Because you have rejected knowledge, I will also reject you as my priests." God does indeed respond, though not in the way many of us have been taught. That's why *Broken and Spilled Out-An Abuse Recovery Journal: Recovering Yourself by K. J. Sharpe* is urgently needed and timely.

I met Ms. Sharpe 22 years after her abusive marriage. When she shared her testimony concerning what she had endured, it genuinely touched my heart. Her story was so similar to mine. She too was raised in a Christian home, attending a church with strict rules and regulations. Wearing red was taboo. Makeup, jewelry, pants, and listening to 'secular' music was forbidden. Questioning church doctrine and established beliefs was strongly discouraged. Hearing her, I promised to be available as her Spiritual Pastoral Care Pastor. Several conversations later, she called me her spiritual mother.

Previously married, Ms. Sharpe met her second husband in church. Despite both being heavily involved in ministry, she endured his controlling, abusive behavior for several years. Encouraged by her pastor, a woman she loved and trusted, to serve, obey, pray, and stay, she committed to doing everything she could to make the marriage work but nothing helped. She continued to reach out for help but felt unheard, betrayed, and ultimately held responsible for her husband's behavior. Finally, she boarded a bus with her five children, traveling over 400 miles to escape what had become an increasingly dangerous environment. By this time, the abuse had escalated and extended to her children. Afterwards, she and her children were ostracized and ignored. The pain her family experienced was deep and devastating.

D.C. Alliance had the opportunity to interview Ms. Sharpe for a virtual broadcast on domestic violence. I learned about gaslighting; a term previously unfamiliar to me. She explains it in this book as a mind control campaign, psychological warfare that leaves victims second-guessing themselves, feeling hopeless, helpless, and crazy without the perpetrator ever touching them. She goes into further detail about how your partner uses the weaknesses they learned in the beginning of the relationship to further manipulate and control personal perception and actions. She shares the history and culture of domestic violence and abuse passed down through the ages. She uncovers how laws, religion, and society continue to impact violence against women. She educates us, removing the masks of toxic religion with the truth about spiritual beliefs that have been used to keep women in bondage. She holds leadership accountable. She teaches on forgiveness and the importance of first forgiving ourselves. She shares her testimony of being the "bent over woman" and how she learned to release the pain and move on, walking "by faith and not by sight." She encourages us to get support, offering resources and recommendations for self-care, emergency hotlines, and community services. She assures us that we don't have to walk the journey of freedom and recovery alone. One powerful statement that touched me the most was from her eldest daughter who said, "Mom I didn't know who you were until we left." It was also amazing to read that she loved her husband, even after all that had transpired. In time, she was able to move on with no animosity, understanding what she had power over and what she didn't.

Ms. Sharpe's story could have ended differently. Her positivity, willingness to forgive, and acceptance of responsibility to advocate for others demonstrates that though she may have been broken, she was not destroyed. No longer bent over, she stands, shares, and lives life abundantly.

I preached a sermon titled, *Will the Real Church Stand Up*, challenging churches to get involved and make a difference. Religious communities can no longer sweep domestic violence under the rug. Our legislative system has failed us. It's broken and desperately in need of repair. Regrettably, domestic violence, sex trafficking, and abuse rose exponentially during the pandemic. We must get involved to make a change including calling our senators about reauthorizing the Violence Against Women Act that has been sitting on the senate floor since 2013.

Once you read *Broken and Spilled Out-An Abuse Recovery Journal: Recovering Yourself*, you will not have any more excuses. You must do something. You must act. Ms. Sharpe teaches us that no matter what position you are in, you can get up, tell the truth, and make a difference. This book will be a best seller.

Pastor Patricia Saunders, M.Div. Th.D.
Spiritual Pastoral Care Advisor

TABLE OF CONTENTS

Introduction: On Letting Go

ON LETTING GO

[From "Sistah, Can You Feel Me" by K. J. Sharpe ©2010]

It takes courage to let go.

Let go of those things familiar

To let people go

Fly or fall

And not feel guilty.

Allowing them

Finally

To be responsible for themselves.

It's hard to let go.

But if we are ever to pursue

And recover all.

We must let go of what is.

Open the hand

That has been fisted tight

To receive something new

And wonderful

And beautiful

Clear our lives of the clutter that is our life

And live

And love

Abundantly

As promised.

Only in letting go

Can the final healing begin.

Only in letting go

Can we

Recover

All

1 *CHAPTER ONE*

Once Upon a Time

Now dreams are not available to the dreamers, nor songs to the singers. In some lands dark night and cold steel prevail. But the dream will come back, and the song break its jail. – Langston Hughes

It has been over twenty years since I left my abusive marriage, my five children in tow. It was the most frightening and rewarding thing I have ever done in my life. It is a choice I will never regret.

There are other women like me, faced with a decision they struggle with, cry over, come to grips with or deny. Do I leave or do I stay and what are the repercussions of both? Who and what will I have to leave behind? What will I have to live without? How will I survive? What lifestyle will I and my children have? Will I be able to take care of my children, myself? All of this is real, but I will begin this entry with a dream.

Once upon a lifetime ago, I fell asleep and into a lucid dream. In the dream, I was pinned to a bed by a man taller and stronger than me. He held me down with the full weight of his long, muscular body. I fought, to no avail, to get away from him, trying to pull my wrists from his vice grip, to remove my limbs from under him. He sneered and mocked me, getting perverse pleasure out of my struggle. He told me repeatedly how helpless, how powerless I was and what he was free to do to me. He told me I would never be able to get away from him. Never be able to escape. No matter how hard I struggled. No matter how hard I tried. I fought him until I was too exhausted to move. No matter how hard I struggled against him, he retained power and control over me.

At some point, I gave up. I stopped fighting him and just breathed. Then something strange happened. The minute I stopped fighting. The moment I took a breath, I got a revelation, an epiphany. I looked squarely, deeply and boldly into the man's eyes and confidently said, "Wait a minute. You are not real. This is a dream, and I can wake up."

When I received and believed the revelation, my captors hold on me weakened. Snatching my hands free, I thrust him away from me and woke up.

When my eyes flew open, I lay still, not sure whether I was still dreaming or living in my reality. This dream and its meaning were abundantly clear to me. A slow, knowing smile spread across my face. I allowed myself the luxury of becoming fully awakened to the epiphany in the dream and the answer I needed for my life.

I was in an abusive marriage. The dream helped me to realize that I was not powerless. That I had believed a lie. Once I realized and acknowledged the lie, I took on the attitude of deliverance and the man's hold on me weakened. There was no knight in shining armor. No one came to my rescue. No other mortal was sent to deliver me. I had recognized for myself that I was living with an illusion, and it was up to me to deliver myself from something that was never meant to be my reality. Deliverance began the moment I confronted the lies with the truth.

Lying in bed, I felt triumphant. I was grateful for the message from the universe. I felt empowered. I knew that I could never again be held captive if I chose to wake up to the truth about my life. I also knew that there would be no one coming to rescue me. My deliverance, my freedom, my way of escape was up to me. I alone had to bear the heavy weight and responsibility of choosing how my life was going to play out from that moment on. As terrifying as that was, it was a responsibility I took seriously. A challenge I knew I was ready for.

That dream was the beginning and ending for me. I knew my marriage was headed for disaster in year four when I asked my husband what he thought the purpose of marriage was. He answered, "A wife is to obey her husband and, if she gets out of line, he is to discipline her." I realized that his philosophy and the social conditioning he had been exposed to from childhood, had settled in him a deep-seated belief that women had no real value, and the marital relationship was where a man exerted dominance over her.

After having the dream, I began executing a plan that took me three years to complete. There were a great many challenges. The scary 450-mile ride on the Greyhound bus fearing for my life and my children's. The fear of getting caught. Contending with the fall out of physical and emotional pain that I and my children struggled through. Homelessness seven times. All of it was hard but we survived and somehow managed to thrive. The collateral beauty was, I recovered my soul. I saved my children's lives.

I am not the only one with this story. I am not the only one with these scars. There are thousands of others who have walked out this journey, who have traversed this path and survived. The unfortunate reality is that too many never make the journey, especially those in faith communities who feel they must choose between their God and their deliverance. Some start and never finish. They are not to be judged. The weight of 'just leaving' is enormously heavy, crushing. Some start but do not survive.

There are no pat answers, no magical solutions, no straightforward way out or through. Every person who is faced with domestic violence and abuse comes to a place where thy must make a choice whether to take the chance and flee, fight for their relationship, or remain and hope and pray that it all works itself out.

Even after the dream, after the revelation, after feeling empowered, I was not immediately ready. My children were the final impetus that shot me forward. Children have no choices. I was the adult. I had to make the final call.

It is possible to defend ourselves against the lie. We must acknowledge the truth of the thing in order to be our big, bold, beautiful selves again. We can recover our souls no matter how damaged, broken and bruised we are.

There is a story in the Bible of David who, after fighting a victorious battle, came home to the Ziklag encampment to find it burned to the ground and all the women and children stolen from the camp. David and his men wept and many of them talked about stoning him. As the story goes, David asked God what to do. Do I pursue, or do I stand here and wait? The answer he received was pursue and recover all. David got everything he went back for and more.

I am advocating that you too pursue. Recover your self-esteem. Recover your power. Recover your life. Recover yourself and your generations. Pursue and recover all.

The Betrayal

This above all: to thine own self be true, and it must follow, as the night the day, thou canst then be false to any man. – William Shakespeare

One thing I have had to come to grips with many times in my life is the act of betrayal. Remembering Judas, I think of my own betrayals to myself. Infinitesimally small and gargantuan duplicitous infidelities I must forgive myself for.

According to scriptures, Jesus was neither surprised nor angered at Judas' betrayal. He loved his friend and knew Judas loved him. Jesus also knew Judas' heart. They had lived together, traveled together, argued, and fought together for a long time. He knew Judas prized money and power more than anything else. He knew Judas was disappointed in Jesus' leadership, a leadership that did not lead to the overthrow of the Roman empire. Jesus expected what came next. He told Judas to go ahead and do what was in his heart (John 13:21-27).

As heartbreaking as the betrayal of a loved one is, the daily betrayals we heap upon ourselves are even more of a hindrance to our lives, battering our self-love into an angry submission. This was the epiphany I had when considering the story of Judas.

I have found myself many times in places doing things I felt I should not have done, betraying what I believed, thought, and felt to be true for want or need. Sometimes it was a matter of course. My children had to eat so I took jobs that I hated rather than follow my bliss. When we lived in a shelter, my children were cold for want of coats, gloves, hats to keep them warm. We had escaped in the summer. The clothing I had snuck away to put in storage, was still in Pennsylvania as we did not yet have a home of our own. Clothing and other goods were donated to the shelter for use by the shelter tenants but was often only distributed to favorites. Everyone else had to work it off.

To earn credits toward the purchase of these donated items, I would take the biggest jobs like cleaning the yard. The bigger the job, the more credits you earned. I was new to the shelter. I didn't have enough credits, nor could I earn them fast enough to buy coats and winter wear before autumn chill or winter cold set in. My job, when I finally got one, paid $5.75 per hour. An extreme drop from the lucrative contracts I had before I left my husband. I was the children's sole provider and protector. I was not going to let them be without because of my decision. Not on my watch. I was going to get them what they needed by any means necessary.

When I first came to the shelter, I was told about a place called "the shed" where all the contributions of clothing, housewares, and home goods were kept. I was warned that people stole things from the shed. I was appalled that someone would commit such a crime in a place where they were being helped. Shelters, sleeping on the floor, and thieves, oh my! How naïve, arrogant, and prideful I was until my children couldn't get what they needed no matter how hard I worked. Frustrated, angry, and tired, I chose to be an accomplice in the grand theft of coats, gloves, boots, socks, pj's, long underwear, hats, hoodies, and scarves from "the shed" where the stockpile of donated items were sorted and stored. I stuffed all these things into three bookbags, also from the shed, and snuck them up to my room where I immediately put them with the children's things as though they had always been there. At first, I felt guilty and ashamed, then angry and frustrated. Why do I have to "buy" what was donated for me and families like me? Why must I be forced to be a criminal in a system where families in situations like mine are subject to even further debasement by those who claim to be their champions? Why must I be forced to choose between betraying my long-held values and putting coats on my children's backs and shoes on their feet?

I betrayed myself in love, taking conditional lovers. Those who loved me because they needed me as opposed to needing me because they loved me. I accepted convenience when I was afraid of commitment. I accepted being an option when I really wanted to be a priority. There were so many times I smiled and said yes when I really wanted to say no and hell no! Times when I have been kind when I really wanted to punch someone in the face. Times when I didn't allow myself the luxury of tears or the release of anger. Times when I hid my pain behind silence, agreement, and people pleasing when I should have cried and screamed out loud. Many times, when I have held parts of my outstanding self in check so other people would feel less intimidated, less small, less inadequate around me.

It is the little betrayals, by and large, that eventually cause our self-imposed, self-inflicted, self-destruction. I am most tired of betraying me.

It can be challenging to keep the promises we make to ourselves. Loneliness, need, lust, anger, and fear get in the way, so we settle. We settle into silence. We settle into acceptance. We settle into acquiescence. We settle because we either believe we don't deserve better or because we have no hope that things can be better or that anything better is out there for us.

I have been, done and believed all those things. It's hard to focus when you are distracted by ever present need. Jesus fed the 5,000 before he spoke a word to them. He knew they could not hear him or receive what he was saying over the insistent grumbling of their bellies or the psychotic ramblings of their minds, so he first addressed their immediate need.

Our needs are reasonable. Our concerns are not without merit. The thing is figuring out what to do, how not to betray ourselves in the face of all of that. We will not always win the battle, but we may in some way win the war we wage against ourselves by learning to stand our ground.

Honoring your commitments to yourself is no easy task. You will have setbacks. You will fall off the wagon, fall over, and fall out repeatedly. It takes practice to be true to yourself and lots of it. You must remember that it is those small betrayals, the little worms, which eat at your soul, sabotaging the fullness of the best of us. But one step at a time, inch by painstaking inch, we can make progress every day in recovering the magnificence of ourselves that we had at the beginning.

Surrender

Esau said…What good is the birthright to me? So, he swore an oath to him, selling his birthright to Jacob. – Genesis 25:29-34; NIV

You can surrender your power or keep it. The choice is always yours. The only thing is, once you give it up, you may have to fight tooth and nail to get it back.

Everyone wants to be loved and accepted. This is a valid human need and desire. That need, however, if we are not careful, can drive us to become sacrificial lambs, martyrs on the altar of our insufficiency.

Esau and Jacob were brothers, Esau the elder, Jacob the younger. Esau sold the rights to his entire inheritance to Jacob for a bowl of soup. His immediate hunger was more important to him than his legacy. Too late, Esau realized that he had surrendered not only his birthright, but the provision for his generations.

What have you surrendered for the sake of your immediate need? What have you given up for a temporary fix? What have you submitted to in exchange for acceptance?

In sacrificing who you are for what you want right now, you become consumed by the immediate. That thing you thought was so important in the moment can detract from the most important thing in your life – time. You only have will power if you will take responsibility and own your power. When you turn your power over to someone, anyone, or anything else, you have prostrated yourself on the altar of a golden calf.

Before you give yourself away, you must know and accept that there is no need for someone else to complete you. You are complete within yourself. You need to be complete and whole before you enter into a relationship. You need to have and recognize your own wholeness before giving away fractions of yourself to other people. The "better half" is a myth and a lie. A half or part of anything is always a fraction, a division or tiny element of the whole. Anything done in fractions is by its very nature fractured, broken down into smaller denominations. Two halves in a relationship can create a whole lot of mess. One will eventually drain the other causing destruction to be its inevitable end.

Learn to hold on for dear life to your personal power and build from there. A solid, self-loving, personal foundation builds a great house, a great relationship, a great family, a great life not just for you but for the generations that follow.

Pampered

You're allowed to ask what serves you. I know you've been trained up to serve everyone. But you're allowed to turn that on yourself and honor your own life that you were given. — Elizabeth Gilbert

Most women spend so much time giving to and serving others, they neglect their own needs. I remember spending one early Friday morning sitting in a high school salon, my feet soaking in hot soapy water, a jet massage soothing the tension and softening the calluses and corns on my rugged toes and the hardened balls of my feet. It had snowed the day before. From my comfortable position, I looked out at the wisps of white blanketing the school's campus, clinging to trees as soft sheets continued to fall. I inhaled and exhaled deeply, relaxed. Despite the classroom full of teenage girls chattering noisily over the loud hum of hairdryers and clacking flat irons, the atmosphere was calming and peaceful.

My eldest daughter was a cosmetology student at that time. The best in her class. Yes, I am proud mama bragging. Elaine (not her real name) is naturally talented, charming, and hysterically funny. I was having my feet done at her school largely because it was her class assignment, and she would rather have taken the zero than touch anybody else's feet. It was a rare bonding experience for us, and we both had a wonderful time.

Self-pampering was something I had become accustomed to neglecting.

The pedicure in Elaine's classroom was the most pleasant experience I had allowed myself in a decade. Elaine had invited me to take the time to sit still for a few hours and allow someone to serve me. Not only did my feet feel refreshed and renewed, so did my spirit.

I have since taught my daughters that self-pampering, self-preservation is not selfish. These things are essential to our wellbeing. Self-care can be simple, a walk in the park or on the beach or down the street and around the corner. Walking helps us to breathe and think. The movement alone generates dopamine in our system which gives us that peace of mind feeling. Walking it out allows you time to get clear. There is something powerful about having our feet on the ground and moving in a direction we choose even if only for five to 15 minutes a day. I have always loved feeling the fresh air on my face, or rain, or a cold breeze touching my cheek as I walk. Nature has a way of offering us succor, of blowing us a kiss at just the right time if we just get out into it. Even if it's just walking around barefoot in the grass in the front of your house or your back yard. Get out and enjoy for your own sake.

Allow yourself to dream. This too is important to the self. Focus on what it is going to be like to live free. What music will you listen to? What kind of friends will you have? What quality of life will you have? Do a vision board in a notebook to keep for yourself. Include pictures of all the wonderful things you would like to have, be, and do in your life. The exercise alone will lift your spirits.

Pampering is more than giving yourself a facial, getting a foot massage, getting your nails and hair done. The word pamper is synonymous with indulgence, attention, comfort, kindness, and catering. How kind, compassionate, loving, and forgiving are you with yourself? What makes you feel good about you? About your life? We ask our kids what they want to be and do when they grow up. We need to keep asking that question of ourselves. What do you want to be? What do you want to do? How can you best serve you?

You have the legal, democratic, and spiritual right and responsibility to defend, protect and serve all that you are. Your dignity, your integrity, your power, your spirit, your body, mind, thoughts, your soul all belong to you. You have the right to say no and enough. You are the border patrol for any attempted coup or terrorist attacks against your person, your spirit, and your will. Abuse, whether verbal, emotional, psychological, sexual, physical, or financial is an outright assault, no matter who does it or their reasoning for doing so. Just as every democratic republic has the right to defend and protect itself, so do you. You are your country.

Self-preservation is not selfish. It is necessary for your survival. Make it your mission not to be overwhelmed by the things so many others expect, demand, and genuinely need from you. Protect yourself and your soul by setting boundaries and building your own territorial walls. It is your God given right to protect and preserve yourself. You are worthy. Do not allow anyone to overcome the kingdom that reigns within you.

Masquerade

We wear the mask that grins and lies. It hides our cheeks and shades our eyes. This debt we pay to human guile. With torn and bleeding hearts, we smile. – Paul Laurence Dunbar

Are we all pretending? We talk about being real but are we really? We make up stories to cover who we are and who we are not. We post pictures on social media that make our lives look happy and peaceful when in truth we are tortured and sad. We lie about who we are in relationship to others and who they are to us. In public forums our "boo" is nothing more than a ghost in real life. On social media we have perfect lives, perfect bodies, perfect jobs, and perfect ideas. In reality, we have no idea who we are, what we want, and why we are here. We pretend well.

We pretend like children playing make believe because we cannot bare the reality of our lives and who or what we are becoming because of it. We wear the mask, shucking and jiving, grinning, and lying while we utter vague empty epitaphs as greetings and farewells.

Why do we choose to shuffle along counting our days by breaths? We watch time slip away from us, our dreams crushed between the palms of our praying hands and poured out like grains of sand running too quickly through an hourglass. Why do we stay in relationships that rob us of our joy, our hope, our faith, and our reason? Too afraid to admit that we have invested so much of our heart and soul stock in the wrong portfolio, we stay. Even when we see our investment continually crash without recovery, plummeting steadily to zero, we sigh and get comfortable with the devil we know. Why do we hide our shame and sorrow in drugs, alcohol and illicit behavior that further devalues us? Crying, screaming, praying we ask our higher power to make it better. We lay prostrate on the floor, begging, pleading for things to change knowing all the while that we must be the change we want to see.

We pretend in order to normalize our chaos, to maintain our sanity. We tell ourselves that everybody lives like this, hungers like this, gets beat up emotionally and physically at one time or another like this, and everything is okay or going to be. That is, until the dam breaks. In an abusive relationship, this can happen at any moment for any reason at any time of the day or night. We try to patch things up with constant compromises, co-dependence, fault finding and blame. We pacify. Lie some more. Hide some more of who we are. We play small so our partner can feel big. We act out the damsel in distress to their superman or vice-versa, losing ourselves a little bit at a time. We become accustomed to the drama, create more of our own, become addicted to it and believe the lie that we cannot live without it.

So, we live afraid, frustrated, sad, and angry. Afraid of and for our children and our lives, we think about escape. We ask the serious questions until, frozen and immobilized by worry and fear, we convince ourselves things are not that bad. Numb, we put on the mask and dance the masquerade, two stepping for our lives.

On average, a woman leaves an abusive relationship seven times before she leaves for good. Abuse is about control. Abusers do not lose control. It is not the drugs or the alcohol or their family history. It's the mask. Controlling behavior, psychological manipulation and physical battery is a meticulously masterful chess game and anyone can be prey or pawn. Acting in a dual personality, abusers gain control by intimidation, gas-lighting, blaming, and making you second guess your own decisions and motives. But the honeymoon faze is all flowers and chocolates, red hearts, and smiley faces. Your abuser becomes a lover, a model parent, a loyal friend, or boyfriend in disguise.

It is not your duty to rip off anyone's mask or to help them heal. It is paramount, however, that you recognize your own fake face, rip it off and say, this is what it is, this is who I am for real. You will have to name the horror that branded you and the person you have become because of it. It will not do for you to blame and hide; that includes blaming and hiding from yourself. Revelation, the knowing how, will never come to you until you stop pretending. If you don't rip off the masks, if you continue to put on more false faces, hiding behind makeup and make-believe, eventually, you will smother yourself to death.

Guilty Feet

Guilty feet have got no rhythm. – George Michael.

I was a dancer and choreographer for more than half my life. Whenever I was preparing to perform, I diligently watched what, when, how, and how much I ate. I never ate a big meal on the day of a performance because it made me feel heavy, weighted down, and fatigued. My body rhythm was thrown off and I didn't perform well. This is also true when we carry guilt. You cannot dance gracefully into your future carrying the weight of guilt from your past.

One of my greatest challenges with parenting has been guilt. When I screwed up and my children were affected, I felt guilty. When I tried to impart wisdom, and they refused to listen and harmed themselves, I felt guilty. I constantly beat myself over the head and berated myself for what I saw as parenting mistakes and missteps. I bemoaned all my wrong choices, bad advice, words I shouldn't have said and those I should have. I spent hours upon hours examining myself, highlighting my every flaw and apologizing to my children for it all. When my children did something wrong, I even apologized for their mistakes as if I had caused the thing and not their decisions.

When you are burdened with guilt, you can't dance. You can't be happy. You feel ashamed of everything you have ever said and done in your life. Nothing about you looks good to you. You feel undeserving and unworthy of the good stuff, the good life. You start speaking more burden and bad tidings into your own existence. You beat yourself up and life stops for you right there because you have, blindly, convinced yourself you don't deserve anything more. Anything better. Depression and hopelessness follow. You fall headfirst into self-pity and victimization which leads to manipulation by your partner and the children you love. This becomes a concentric circle spinning like an out-of-control Ferris wheel.

A family counselor brought my guilt to the forefront. She had quietly observed my interactions with one of my children. She saw that the child used my feelings of guilt to get me to give in to her demands. It was a very subtle and highly effective manipulation. The counselor warned me that if I did not change my behavior, all the other children would begin to challenge me in the same way and I would, as she said, "have a full blown mutiny on my hands."

Of course, I didn't want to hear it. I wanted to shoot the messenger and gave no credence to a 29-year-old young woman with book learning and no children of her own. I ignored the message. She was challenging me to find out what I got out of holding onto guilt. I dismissed her.

But I couldn't shake the question. First, I beat myself up again. In my mind, a stranger could see I was a bad mother making mistakes again. I wanted to be the perfect parent. I was trying to make up for all the things I felt I had robbed my children of. I held myself responsible for all the mistakes I and their fathers had made.

When I finally faced myself, it was tough to admit that if I held on to the guilt, I could be the good guy. I could be the martyr, the suffering saint. I was still dealing with feelings of rejection, abandonment, and insecurity from my childhood. I was looking for love, acceptance, and affirmation from my children. I felt guilty about taking them out of their former unsafe environment and placing them into another one that was not particularly stable. I felt guilty about not being able to give them what they wanted and sometimes what they needed. I tried to compensate for the "sins of the fathers" by giving them things I could not really afford, bending over backwards and going the extra mile. They knew I felt bad about what had happened to us and some of them in their teen years, would not let me forget it. I accepted blame for everything, whether it was my fault or not. I was used to accepting it. I had years of experience and training carrying other people's weight.

Once I faced down my guilt, I had to deal with the truth. I was furiously angry. Carrying all that stuff that was not mine gave my anger justification. At the same time, it gave me some weird sense of control. My anger allowed me to hold stuff over people's heads and make them feel guilty too. It was a hollow reward.

The first step to recovery for me was acknowledging that I was mad at everybody! My former spouses, my children, my family, my church, and the entire male species. I was angry with God and the whole host of heaven. I was mad I had to suppress my anger because some of the people I was angry with not only had more power than me, but they also had power over me. I was afraid they had enough power to destroy me and my children's lives. I was angry about feeling powerless, hopeless, helpless, and impotent. I was angry about being poor, about suffering and struggling while both my former spouses progressed exponentially in their lives.

For an entire month or more, after the encounter with the counselor, I boiled over with anger. I went out to an open field and screamed until my throat hurt. I went down to the beach and screamed at the waves at sunrise, throwing stones and handfuls of dry sand. I talked to a friend and screamed. I stood on a grassy median in the middle of a busy intersection and screamed at the top of my lungs. I did not care if I looked like a crazy woman. I was angry and the whole universe was going to know it. I had been carrying anger for so long it was lethal.

I had to learn to let people carry their own weight. I had to learn how to say no and enough. I had been a people pleaser and makeup artist for decades in the name of acceptance. I had to learn to accept myself, flaws and all. I wanted everybody in my world to be happy even if it meant I was miserable. I had to accept that I deserved to be happy too and the responsibility for that was on me.

I had to learn to set boundaries. I felt used and worn out because I had never set any boundaries for me. I was not a priority to myself. What everybody wanted and needed was more important than anything I ever wanted or needed. This was strongly disproportionate. Parenting involves sacrifice, not martyrdom. This too I had to learn.

I wanted my children to have a good life and I blamed myself for not being able to give them the kind of life I had imagined for them. I believed children should be happy, feel loved and have stability. We were living in hotels and motels along the beach and getting free food on a weekly basis from a church when I didn't have a job. When I did finally get a place, there never seemed to be enough of anything. The money always ran out before the month no matter how hard or how many jobs I worked. I felt so bad for never having enough.

I was so consumed with what my children didn't have that I didn't notice them growing into more compassionate people. I overlooked the fact that they were more mature and more able to deal with hardship than most of their peers. I wasn't even cognizant of their persistence, gratitude, determination, and fortitude until I stepped back from the guilt. The suffering, the struggle, did not just make me stronger. It had cultivated strength and fortitude in them too!

I did not do everything right. No parent does. Neither did I do everything wrong. I have learned that a failed marriage does not mean that I am a failure. Marriage is a joint venture. It may only take one to be dissatisfied, but it takes two to make it work. I was only part of the equation, not the whole. I had to take responsibility for my part and only my part.

I had to accept that my children were not displaced because I was a bad mother. They were displaced because I had made the wise and difficult choice to leave a bad situation. We weren't struggling because I was lazy or inadequate. We were struggling for lack of adequate support.

There are some things I still get angry about, but I no longer suppress or hold that anger. I acknowledge it, confront the person or situation, and deal with it as best I can. My children are now grown and responsible for their own choices. I have apologized for my mistakes, but I do not carry anything they may refuse to forgive me for because I have forgiven myself.

I have learned that no matter what you do, you cannot make everything better. You cannot want something more for someone than they want for themselves, no matter how much you love and care for them. I have also learned that trying to manipulate people's emotions by guilt tripping and blaming is not healthy and will result in a very shaky and distrustful relationship at best.

Guilty feet have got no rhythm and since I love to dance, I am learning to lay aside the weight cause, let's face it, we all miss the mark. We have all shot our arrows and fallen short of the bull's eye. I cannot dance carrying other people's stuff. I cannot leap under a weight of condemnation. What I have learned is to face my demons, throw off the weight, and dance!

<u>Me, Myself, and I</u>

I love myself when I am laughing. And then again when I am looking mean and impressive. – Zora Neale Hurston

If tis a virtue to love thy neighbor as a human being, it must be a virtue -and not a vice-to love myself since I am a human being too. – Erich Froman

I believe that when you love yourself, you automatically and by default, love your source. To love the creation, to nurture it, find joy in it, live peaceably with it is the highest love you can attain in this life. What sense does it make to love thy neighbor and hate thyself? You are your closest neighbor, inseparable, one.

I have had to learn to love myself time and again. To recognize how unbelievably valuable and priceless I am. I have been called dirty names, and answered to those names – bitch, whore, stupid. Sometimes the name calling was subtle. "I don't know what you were thinking. Do you use your brain?" or "What's wrong with your brain?" At one time in my life, I accepted those words and grew to believe them as I heard them repeated. Love had been used as a weapon to indict me, disempower me, and distract me from my purpose, my ambition, my dreams, and my destiny.

When I was growing up, girls were expected to be demure, chaste, and amenable. There was a little ditty that said girls were made of "sugar and spice and everything nice." In my mother's house, girls wore dresses, sat with ankles crossed, legs to the side, and served. It was an extremely strict Christian home. So much so that the first time I bought a pair of pants and wore them in my mother's house, I was called rebellious and on-your-knees family prayer swiftly followed.

Women and girls, especially in religious communities, were never encouraged to talk about their great escapes. Even when their hearts were breaking. Even when they were verbally, physically, sexually, and otherwise assaulted.

This thinking, this type of socialization, has led to a great deal of harm to women and children internationally. This idea that we are to be neither seen nor heard. That our voices, when heard, do not matter, and should be sanctioned. That when we speak, plan, stand up and make a difference, we are "ball busters" and "bitches." People who lead the march and make noise, looked in the mirror one day, reflected on their journey and said, I am going to stand up and make a change. That kind of confidence requires first and foremost the love and acceptance of self.

If I am to love God, Source, Infinite Intelligence, I must first love me; for to love the created thing, is to love the creator. We get self-love all twisted and out of order. Self-love is not selfish. Women especially have been trained to honor and esteem everyone before themselves and like it. This kind of bondage warps our perception. We begin to count ourselves unworthy of the love we seek and selfish for asking for and pursuing it. We accept what we do not want and deny our desires. We settle for less and feel undeserving and ashamed for wanting more. Slowly, innocuously our self-worth diminishes, and our self-esteem disintegrates. We annihilate ourselves, our dignity, and our self-respect.

I do not feel the original plan of God/Source has changed. We are all created from love, created to be loved, to give and receive love. No matter what religion, what faith, or lack thereof, no matter what doctrine you believe or espouse, the fact remains loving ourselves is paramount to loving our neighbor.

"Love thy neighbor as thyself" implies that respect for one's own integrity and uniqueness, love for and understanding of oneself, cannot be separated from respect, compassion, love, and understanding for another indivdual. The love you give is equal to the love of and for yourself which is inseparably connected with the love for any other living thing.

Every child is born in oneness, a distinct creation entering the world alone. No matter how many a mother carries in her womb, each child is birthed one at a time, alone. All one. Complete. To be whole and healed we must first come to a place of loving ourselves alone.

Play Nice

There are still huge swaths of women who never got the memo that their lives belong to them. — Elizabeth Gilbert

When we were children, we would get into a fight with a sibling, a child at school, the neighborhood bully, or our best friend. An adult would break up the fight and tell us to play nice.

As an adult, I have since been on both sides of the play nice spectrum. What I have learned is that you cannot expect people to play nice when they know you are being abused. They do not understand why you are allowing or engaging in the madness that is your life. They want you to get it together, wise up, and stand up for yourself. They do not understand the psychosis that comes with verbal and physical abuse. They do not understand, and you cannot make them. You can't make them because you are too busy giving excuses, trying to reason and hide your own reality, even from yourself. You can't make them understand because you don't understand, because you are ashamed, because you are afraid. They want to help you, but on their terms. You want help, but only on your terms. You do not want to be judged, screamed at, or ridiculed. These are the people that love and care about you and they are frustrated, angry, and afraid. You have tied their hands and they do not know what to do for you. If you are a person who goes from one abusive relationship to another, they are fed up with rescuing you. Calls in the middle of the night, emergency family meetings, and altercations with your significant other wreak as much havoc on their lives as yours. They want to know when the roller coaster ride is going to be over, when the drama you are absolutely unable to live without is going to stop interfering with the peace they are trying to find in their own lives.

Abuse is never done in a vacuum. It affects everyone including you, your significant other, your children, siblings, parents, friends, and community. You are mad at family and friends for saying or not saying something, for doing and not doing something, for caring or not caring enough to say, feel, or do anything. You are angry because of their inability or unwillingness to rescue you in the way you want them to or think they should.

You keep living in your fantasy bubble to avoid confrontation but life, real life, is not a fantasy. Your dream guy or girl has turned into a monster, and you think if you love them enough and in the right way, the monster will change back into the prince or princess. You want the great host of witnesses to your life to believe the same thing, to live the lie with you.

News flash, people only change when they feel the need to. The honeymoon phases you experience are only short, sweet, make-believe scenarios that lull you into a false sense of security. There will come a day when your family and friends do not want to pretend with you anymore. They want to get off your fantasy island and most of them will. They will stop associating with you, calling, and visiting which plays to your abuser's secret weapon, isolation. Abusers thrive in creating the drama that ensures your loved ones will desert you. It is part of the plan.

There is an end goal.

It is not your fault that you are being abused. You must recognize and acknowledge, however, that there is nothing you can do that will change who and what your abuser is. You cannot love them enough, serve them enough, be kind enough, loving enough, sexy enough. You cannot be enough for a person whose only goal is to make you feel less than and to have power over you.

The only person you can have any lasting influence over is you. You can stop pretending it is not or has not happened. You can decide not to be servile and people pleasing. You don't have to play nice.

I am a strategist. I have a knack for planning and execution. I am also analytical by nature, listening, watching, and feeling things out for understanding. I take time to assess a situation, weight my options, and execute. That is what was necessary for me to leave my abusive situation. I could not keep hiding or even talking about the abuse anymore. I had to do something if I was going to preserve my life and my children's lives. If something had happened to my children because I could not find the courage to move on, it would have been an impossible weight for me to carry.

Life is complicated. There are no easy solutions to complex problems. Abuse is complicated. An abuser is a bully and when there is a bully on the playground, he does not care about playing nice. He has studied you and knows your weaknesses and your flaws. He knows where you are the most sensitive, what things trouble you, what things you feel guilty about. He or she has no qualms about kicking you when you're down or going for the jugular in public or in private. You can try to stand up to the bully in hand-to-hand combat but that is never going to be a fair fight. You have to be strategic, take away his or her target, and hit them where it counts. You will need help to change the paralysis of analysis into movement. The National Coalition Against Domestic Violence at 1-800-SAFE (7233) enables you to talk to someone anonymously to get questions answered, learn about safety planning, restraining orders, assistance for immigrants and native Americans, or to vent. If you are in Delaware County or the surrounding areas in Pennsylvania, the Domestic Abuse Project of Delaware County's 24-hour hotline, 610-565-4590, and Women Organized Against Rape, 24-hour hotline, 215-985-3333, are also valuable resources. More resources are available in the Resource Guide at the end of this book.

I highly and often recommend therapy for persons in and out of abusive relationships. Make sure, however, when you receive any type of counseling, your therapist or counselor listens without judgement, is certified in trauma informed care, and is someone you are comfortable speaking with. The person should have a genuine interest in you as a human being, respect your boundaries, and be culturally aware. If you are affiliated with a religious organization, I personally recommend you seek help outside of your congregation. My husband and I were involved in Christian counseling at our church. The counselor preferred my husband and did not listen to me, going so far as to tell me to be quiet during a session and afterwards. Make sure you are being heard. You matter. Your voice matters. Partner counseling in abusive relationships is often ineffective. Get a counselor for yourself by yourself and one for your children as well. There are excellent spiritual counselors that have a flexible world view and are not stuck in an ideology of patriarchal roles for men and women. Ask your doctor for recommendations.

Search out the available resources in your community. A woman I know met a female pastor of a small storefront church who hid her and her five children in the church basement. The pastor and her congregation helped the woman and her family not only flee her abuser, but found safe housing, a job, and a car for the mother and her family. A lady who was a stranger to me, helped my family and I with housing, daily meals, and furniture. A church I had never attended paid the deposit for my first month's rent. If you take the leap, the net will often appear, even if you fall a ways before seeing it.

You are the decision maker in your situation. You alone control whatever you deem necessary to protect yourself and your children. Whether you decide to go or stay, prosecute or not, you will need a strategic plan and the wisdom of community for keeping yourself and those you love safe, instituting and protecting boundaries, knowing your limitations, and drawing your line in the sand.

Women learn and have been socially conditioned to play nice. That is why we do not want our significant others to go to jail when we know that is their deserved fate. That is why we justify their behavior. That is why we try to see the good in them. That is why we love them and blame ourselves when they disrespect us, abuse us, sexually assault us. We want to play to what they say they want and need but, in the game, want and need are never fulfilled. We hope in our heart of hearts that they will play nice with us like they did when we first met them. We live for the honeymoon phase but the longer we are in the game, the more infrequent the honeymoon occurs. People exhibiting abusive behaviors are not interested in playing nice with you. They get off by hurting you. That is what turns them on.

You may not have the courage to do anything about your situation right now. That's all right. When you examine your truth, you may find that it is fear that keeps you there, not love. That is normal and natural too. You may have become addicted to the drama or be so entrenched in your partner's family; you don't want to disconnect yourself and especially your children from people they know and love. That's understandable. You may believe on some level that the abuse is what you deserve, that you are unworthy, that no one else will want you, that you are somehow damaged goods. Because of the psychological damage, this too makes sense. You may be a pillar of your community, attached to the house and way of life, reluctant to give up the finer things. Those feelings are valid. If you understand and connect with the reality of your situation, not make excuses for it, and accept the truth of what it is, you are halfway there. You cannot work on or heal from stuff you do not acknowledge.

At one point during my marriage, I looked in a bathroom mirror after washing my face, and I didn't recognize me. Who was the woman staring back at me with that darkness in her face, the deadness in her eyes, her mouth turned down? Who was the woman in the drab denim shirt and baggy jeans? I despised denim. I was shocked at my own appearance. My hair was falling out. I didn't bother with makeup or jewelry. I didn't smile. What had I become? I had played nice and lost me. For a long time, I believed and lived out the lie that I wasn't worthy, I was unattractive, unwanted, and unlovable. I was a fading shadow of who I once was. That day I told the woman in the mirror, "It's not going down like this. I'm not going out like this."

The journey to recovering me was hard and long. It had me on the floor in tears. I loved my husband. I did not want to leave him. I was terrified, conflicted, and feeling like a failure. This was my second marriage and I wanted more than anything for it to work. I asked God if I should go or stay and the answer clearly for me was, "If you go, I'll be with you. If you stay, I'll be with you." God did not make the decision for me. I had made the decision to get into this marriage. I had to make the decision to stay or get out.

I never felt courageous when I left. I never felt like the hero my children called me in later years. I did not feel confident about leaving. I left in such a hurry that I forgot the meals I had so painstakingly prepared for my children so they wouldn't be hungry on the journey. I wanted to go back many times. I had become addicted to the drama and was going through withdrawal from it. I wanted my old life back, the safety and security of my old friends and family, a home of my own instead of constantly living in cheap motels and the confines of a shelter.

When I look back at all of it, the homelessness, the frequent moves, the stress and hardship, I can honestly say I will never regret my decision. I believe with all my heart and everything in me that it was one of the best decisions I have ever made in my life. My children turned out to be loving, compassionate, good human beings. My eldest daughter said, "Mom, I didn't know who you were until we left." I had blossomed into myself again, a new improved version of me. Leaving was the most loving decision I could have ever made for myself, my children, and my husband.

Domestic violence has a ripple effect and no one around you will go untouched. You do not have to follow your mama's advice and play nice. Play strategic. Play honest. Play using your head and your heart. Play full out. The etymology or original meaning of the word nice is fool.

2 *CHAPTER TWO*

<u>Choose Life</u>

I have set before you life and death, blessing and cursing. Therefore, choose life that both thou and thy seed may live. – Deuteronomy 30:19 (KJV)

Destiny is not a matter of chance; it is a matter of choice. – William Jennings Bryan

Some people go from year to year doing the same things. Because they have the ability, the talent, and the necessary skills or because they are convinced that this is what they have to do, they never make changes. Instead, they fall prey to the defeatist adage, "that's just how it is." Like dogs returning to their own vomit, they lap up the attitude of defeat, hating its bilious smell and ingesting it anyway. Eventually, inevitably, sick and dulled from this acrid poisoning of mind, body, and spirit, they become citizens of the colony of the living dead. This inheritance they pass down from generation to generation with statements like, "You'll never be...," and "I tried that and..."

I don't believe people are fated to a certain lifestyle. Fate is often a product of our own decisions and choices. If fate alone commanded the direction of our lives, then what would be the point of free will or a brain from which to exercise that will. Many a man, woman and child have chosen to arise from the state they were born to, the country that oppressed them, the circumstances that confronted them, the heartache that snatched their very soul. They have chosen to rise above it, like the phoenix from its own ashes.

I agree that sometimes life deals us a really lousy hand. I've been dealt quite a few of them myself. You still have a choice. You can fold. You can play your hand, or you can fight. The decision is, in my opinion and experience, never an easy one. Still, every day we choose. We choose by what we do, what we think, what we say, all the time attracting to us the life we do and do not want.

We are all equipped to live life abundantly whatever abundance looks like to us. I have learned that if you want abundance, if you want to come out of the dark and live in the light, the first thing you have to do, the most difficult step you have to take is to choose. Am I going out like this? Is this the end for me? If it is, what's the last mark I want to make? If today is all I have, what will I choose today? If I'm going to go out, am I going to go out fighting or do I play dead until the funeral?

Make the most of every moment, every second of your life. Choose to live out who you are. Choose your abundance. Think it, speak it, and say it every day. You have more power than you know. Make the choice to use your power.

Subject: To Change

Insanity is doing the same thing over and over again and expecting different results. – credited to Albert Einstein.

Life has a consistent ebb and flow. The sun rises and sets. Flowers bloom and die. Humanity is birthed and buried. Nothing and no one ever gets out of this earth realm alive. Life on earth and under the sun, in all its consistencies, is also always in a state of flux, moving and changing at will whether the will is that of a higher power or man's own hand. Anything that grows must change. Anything that doesn't grow, doesn't change, stagnates, and dies.

I find it amazing that oceanographers are still discovering new life in the dark recesses of the sea, going to depths they have never been before. Astrologists and astronomers who study the galaxies testify that new stars are continually born, composed of an eternal fire. Trees shed leaves and drop seeds that are scattered abroad to blossom in areas unknown. There is a consistency to life that revolves around change.

So it is with us. We all possess the will and the ability to change if we so desire, but desire eludes many of us. Desire is an essential ingredient. It is that strong pressing need that overwhelms us and inspires us to act. It is the reason we toss and turn and stay up at night till our dreams are realized. Desire sets the will in motion and gives us the courage to act. Desire is the fuel that motors us into change. Change occurs only where and when powerful desire is present. You have to want something so strongly you can't live without it in order to generate the necessary energy to get something more. You want a strong marriage; you may have to fight for it. You want a better life; you will have to define that and passionately pursue it. You want to be financially free, you will have to determine "what's in your wallet?"

Nothing comes through this life without the labor pains of change. That strong marriage may mean leaving the abusive one you are in. That better life may mean giving up all the material comforts you now have and own. Financial freedom may mean dealing with the truth about how you handle money.

You can pray and believe all you want but until you are willing to put your desire into motion, until you are willing to act, until you change, everything in your life will remain the same. Day in, day out. Sun rise, sun set. You cannot just pray your way out of an abusive relationship. You will have to do something. If you must pray, make sure your feet are also moving. You can't just jump and shout your way into a better life. Do something and be grateful and joyful along the way. Financial freedom is not coming from your name it and claim it rhetoric without the necessary action. Money really doesn't grow on trees, nor will it drop down from the sky. If you want something different to happen, if you want to be free from the insanity, you have to commit to change.

I believe God, the Universe, Source, Spirit, whatever you want to call your higher power, wants to do a new thing in our lives but nothing can happen if we are unwilling to adjust. Change direction. Adjust your attitude. Amend your perceptions. Renew your mind. Act step by step. Even baby steps count for something.

Denial River

There's a freedom that comes with deliverance that you must secure for yourself. – Bishop T. D. Jakes

In order to secure your freedom, you have to first admit you are in bondage. Denial is a jailer and a cruel warden. She keeps the door open, but never lets you walk through. One of the saddest things to watch is good people dying in Denial River.

We stay too long in relationships that do not serve us. We deny our addictions, abusive behaviors, unhealthy habits, lies we've told ourselves and others. We just keep going under, in so deep we won't even admit we're drowning. We reject help from the people and opportunities sent to our rescue. Too proud, scared, or ashamed to reach out and take hold of the life raft called help. That is when we die.

Pride, fear, and shame are brothers. Triplets born in the same womb; they link arms to destroy the best of us. They conspire to keep us from admitting our wrong choices, unhealthy habits, mistakes, and missteps. They keep us from attaining that childlike vulnerability that is essential to our healing, our hope, and our happiness. They cloak us in dark robes and keep us from attaining the light of day, the glory that we are and have evolved from, the greatness that we were destined for from the foundation of the world. As long as we deny our issues, we will remain in mourning, sitting unnecessarily in sackcloth among the ashes. The breaking of day only arises when we admit our faults, failures, shortcomings, ask for help and act in full faith.

The best way to finally get out of denial river is to look at yourself and your situation and say, this is how it is for real. I'm an addict for real. I'm co-dependent for real. My relationship is unhealthy for real. I'm angry for real. I'm narcissistic, selfish, tired, a people-pleaser, self-righteous, a pain in the ass for real. This abuse, neglect, mistreatment, betrayal is tearing me apart and is not a figment of my imagination. It's real and I have got to do something about it besides crying in the closet and hiding from people who genuinely love and care about me.

You have to admit and face all that is. According to ancient scripture, Jesus himself asked a man, "Wilt thou be made whole" (John 5:6)? That man had to choose to face his condition and how he was handling it. Then he had to choose whether or not he wanted to get out of the place where he was begging, to a new place of freedom and empowerment.

Will you choose to keep drowning or get the hell out of the river? Everybody knows it is useless to do CPR on a dead man.

Frosting

Freedom is just frosting on someone else's cake, and so must be till we learn to bake. —
Langston Hughes

In America today, there is a lot of talk about liberty and justice. What it
is. What we should do about it. Who deserves it? How we can, should,
could obtain and protect it. Global *Black Lives Matter* protests
demanding change speak to the systemic racism, violence, and injustice
against Black people, especially Black males, across the United States
and the world. Tearing down statues built in support of white supremacy
sparks arguments of whether or not these statues should be on public
grounds or in history museums. The debate begs the question of
whether or not we will tell the truth about history, the southern
confederacy, slavery, the execution of free Black men, the theft of land
and property by angry whites. Then there is the confusion concerning
patriotism and the democratic process as demonstrated by the
horrifying, violent storming of the United States Capitol during the
certifying of votes. The shock and terror captured live for the entire
world to see.

Freedom is not a given. The children of Soweto in South Africa paid for
freedom from apartheid with their lives. Nelson Mandela spent 30 years
in prison in the name of freedom. Sojourner Truth, Dr. Martin Luther
King Jr., the Freedom Riders, the founding fathers of the United States of
America all fought and died for this intangible thing we call freedom.
Freedom is not free. It will cost you something.

No one who was ever released from the shackles of bondage, asked for
their freedom. They took it by force. If you are to be free, you must first
know what that means and what it looks like for you then you must
demand it for yourself and your generations. Know that demanding
freedom, casting off the shackles that have you bound, is going to cost

you something. In your heart of hearts, what do you want? What do you believe? Why do you believe it? What are you willing to give up or hold on to? What are you willing to defend with your life? Standing up for yourselves and others will cost you. What price are you willing to pay?

Freedom from the tyranny of toxic religion cost me leaving people I knew and loved. It cost me friendships and relationships that had been extremely important to me. Standing up for myself was scary. I was shaking in my boots, but I made some crucial life changing decisions anyway. I realized that I had given people control over my life, my emotions, my creativity. I had sold my soul for acceptance. Getting all of this back was my responsibility. I was the one who had allowed others to convince me that it was in my best interest to give myself away. Letting go and living life on my own terms was worth everything I had to give up in the process.

As a liturgical dancer and choreographer, people have often tried to pigeonhole me into doing what they thought was best or most appropriate for me. I wouldn't allow anyone to force me into one type or style of dance when I knew how creative and powerful the universal language of dance is. I stood my ground and, as a result, my dancing was banned from some places and given free voice in others.

My grandfather used to say if you don't stand for something, you'll fall for anything. There are people who are standing up in the courts, in the streets, on social media, all over the world demanding change and justice. Freedom isn't free. It costs something. Freedom is not only baking the cake, as in Langston Hughes' poem, it's choosing all the ingredients. What kind of cake do you want? What are you putting into the mix? Freedom necessitates grappling with history, fear, discontent, anger, and injustice.

You will never attain freedom until you act. Stay and pray if that is what you believe in but know that is not the only choice biblically, spiritually, or logically. Catherine Clark Kroeger and Nancy Nason-Clark express this in their book, *No Place for Abuse- Biblical & Practical Resources to Counteract Domestic Violence.*

"Sometimes victims are encouraged to endure abuse as Jesus did. We need to make a differentiation between his voluntary suffering to procure our redemption and his ability in other situations to defend himself against verbal abuse (Mk 3:22-30; Jn8:48-59) and the threat of violence (Lk 4:28-30; Jn 8:59; 10:31-39). Being a doormat in an abusive situation is not following the example of Jesus"(Kroeger & Nason-Clark, 2001, pg 98).

In the book of Mark, the teachers of the law were calling Jesus the devil and he clapped back. In the book of John, Jesus claps back again when he is accused of being a demon possessed Samaritan. The relationship between Jews and Samaritans was fraught with prejudice on both sides. This time when people didn't like what Jesus said, "they picked up stones to stone him." Jesus had the good sense to slip away and protect himself. Then, at the Feast of Dedication, Jesus goes to Jerusalem. He is asked whether he is "the Christ" and again, the teachers did not like his answer. Once again, they picked up stones. Jesus said, (paraphrased), "Now wait a minute. If you don't believe me, believe in the miracles." They said, "Nah man. We do believe the miracles. We ain't stoning you for that. We don't like what you said." Jesus said, "Yo, you mad at me because I said me and God are one? Dude, he called ya'll little gods too! What's up?" They picked up the stones and Jesus got ghost.

According to the book of Luke, at the very start of his ministry, the people Jesus had grown up with, loved, and respected rejected his teachings. His life was threatened in his own hood, Nazareth. They were so mad at him they took him to a cliff to throw him off. According to the scriptures, Jesus just walked right through the crowd and went on about his business like "I ain't fooling with ya'll."

Circumstances may not immediately change. Domestic violence, partner abuse, unfair and unequal treatment of women historically in the United States and abroad, prejudice, and racism have not varied much in their intent and scope. Neither the circumstances nor the appearance of things can prevent you from changing, growing, moving forward if that is what you desire.

It has been 22 years since I left my abusive marriage. The cost was astronomical emotionally, physically, economically, and psychologically. The damage that was done still reverberates down through my generations. I was willing to pay the price because my freedom and that of my generations meant that much to me. Freedom was more than just frosting. It was the whole damn cake!

Dare to Dream

Hold fast to dreams, for if dreams die, life is like a broken winged bird that cannot fly. — *Langston Hughes*

The future belongs to those who believe in the beauty of their dreams.— *Eleanor Roosevelt*

I never did sip daintily at life. I always gulped. Took life in large greedy slabs and gobbled it whole.

As a child, I was quiet, reserved, and shy but none of this was true in my imagination. In my mind, I was the better half of Bonnie and Clyde, the strong, independent woman I read about in romance novels, the adventurous movers and shakers I learned about in history class. In my mind and heart, I was the phoenix, the warrior, the business mogul, the badass, the shooting star that lit up the sky. For a long time, all of this stayed quietly packed away in my mind. But oh, what a feeling it was when some of these dreams finally came to life.

I remember the feeling of holding my first published book, *Sistah, Can You Feel Me,* in my hands. I had self-published it long before I knew what the term self-publishing meant. I had my work bound and printed at a Kinko's copy store. The final copies came in a royal blue box. I remember walking to the car with that precious blue box in my hand, my heart racing, my hands shaking and a big smile on my face. I sat in the car alone, took a deep breath and, in a moment of complete silence, stared at that square of cardboard that held a lifetime of dreams. When I opened it and saw my name on the cover of a simple spiral bound book, fat tears coursed their way down my face onto my neck as I ugly cried.

I'll never forget that moment. I finally felt like the writer I had dreamed of becoming all my life. It didn't matter to me that no big-name publisher had signed me. What mattered was that I had taken some of the hundreds of pages of poetry, prose, and essays I had written, organized them, and put them in a cohesive form I could share with the world. That was tremendous accomplishment for me! It had taken me years to complete the project and I was proud of myself. I was thrilled to my forty-year-old bones. Several years later, I felt the same thrill when I published *Sistah, Can You Feel Me* in paperback and again when I got a five-star rating on Amazon. It didn't matter that I didn't make a bestseller list or how many copies I sold. It mattered that I achieved something great to me! It mattered that people read my writing and were inspired by it. It mattered that I felt as though I was fulfilling the thing I came to earth to do.

Writing cost me hours and hours of concentrated effort and thought.

Rewrite after rewrite, edit after edit, year after year. It cost me financially to the tune of thousands of dollars. I didn't have any money stashed away. I saved and used my income tax money to produce what I wanted. It cost me emotionally as well. It cost me in tears, anxiety, exposure. I had never shared my personal writings in book form before *Sistah, Can You Feel Me*. I had performed some of my work before small audiences since I was a kid but with *Sistah*, I was allowing myself to be naked for the entire world to see.

When we were children, our parents asked us what we wanted to be as grown-ups. We answered with our dreams. Even if that dream was just to be alive. What is your childhood dream? Have you hidden it, put it aside, discarded it? Don't forget to dream. You had a vision for your life. What was it? If you don't have or never had a vision, it's time to create one. Develop a vision board even if you have to keep it a secret. See yourself as the person you want to be. See yourself in the place you want to live, how you want to live. Unpack your dreams. Think outside of your current situation. Get out of your head and out of the box.

It is not lack of power that holds us back. It is often that we cannot see any further than where we are at the moment. Without vision, people perish. Amaze yourself by daring to dream.

3 *CHAPTER THREE*

<u>It's Not in the House</u>

Thus says the Lord: heaven is my throne, and the earth is my footstool. What kind of house would you build for me? And what kind can be my resting place? – Isaiah 66:1-2 (KJV)

In this United States of America, we are blessed to be able to celebrate the freedom of religion. Some of us, and I would venture to say a vast majority of women, need freedom from religion. Many religious leaders, both male and female, by their words and their actions, espouse a philosophy of gender bias that supports domestic violence and terrorism on the home front.

Women, for example, are often told to keep quiet about their great escapes. They are held captive, imprisoned by false doctrine that admonishes them to silently endure their most painful hardships with joy. The most beloved saint of the church is the woman who has suffered long with a smile on her face and kept quiet about it.

I grew up in a community of black churches and, like many black churches across the nation, especially in the south, each had its own building fund. The building fund was money set aside to build things. If the church needed a new air conditioner, heating system, a new roof, or a sign over the building, the money could come from the building fund. A new nursery, learning center, day care could also come from finances in the building fund. Historically this is how black churches were the forerunners in building schools, banks, housing, businesses, and even medical facilities in black communities. These were not megachurches but homegrown community and storefront churches that accomplished great things for the communities they served.

The focal point of the church is the sanctuary. The word sanctuary is synonymous with safety. No matter your spiritual beliefs, nationality, race, sexuality, or creed, the sanctuary should be a place where you are safe. It should be a place where you can reflect, meditate, seek support, and wise counsel. During the civil rights movement, the church was a safe space for people to meet, discuss issues, and develop plans to address them. It was a place of social engagement and service to the community. Unfortunately, in the age of the megachurch and in smaller churches aiming to be mega, the word sanctuary no longer applies. Cases of rape, child molestation, physical, verbal, and emotional abuse in an environment of intimidation, fear, and spiritual extortion exists in its place.

I am not a theologian, but what stands out to me about Jesus and the apostles is that they spent most of their time building people's lives. I am not a minister, pastor, or priest, but I distinctly remember reading about Jesus healing the sick, feeding the hungry, raising the dead, admonishing, teaching, encouraging, and demonstrating love, having no one place to lay down his head and rest. I distinctly remember reading about the disciples and followers of "the way" that Jesus espoused, going from house to house fellowshipping and "having all things in common" with one another, sharing what they had. I am not a bishop or church leader, but I do remember reading that the church was not a building but a community of people who loved, supported, and cared for one another.

There is nothing wrong with having a lovely building or a building fund. I am not insinuating that having a place of worship or being a good steward in the maintenance and expansion of it is a terrible thing. What I am saying is what the Bible says so we don't get the truth and the purpose of things distorted. Salvation is not in the house we build for God. I know that's a pretty bold statement. It is not in the shiny gold of the tabernacle. It's not in the heavy velvet curtains, the cushioned pews, or the most up-to-date sound system. It is not in the fold out chairs, pastors' robes, or the pulpit. It's not in the programs we design or the numbers who attend. It is not in the house. There is no edifice you can ever build that will bring as much glory to God as when you commit to build people.

When churches get so busy about a building that they forget about the individuals in the building, they become ineffectual tabernacles. It is God who then takes up the laments of those the church has left wounded, broken hearted, beaten, and impotent with sorrow. I don't believe God really cares about how often we pray or go to church, which church we go to, or whether or not we go to church at all if our lives aren't positively affecting people. Being fruitful and multiplying is about so much more than procreation. It is about recreating the love in which we were created. If that's not in the house we build for God, then what's the point?

It is not in the house. God is too vast to live in a building. Heaven cannot contain the presence, the immeasurable light and love that the entire universe holds. We were all created from this source.

It's not in the house. God isn't overly concerned about the air conditioning, how many square feet of space we do or do not have, or whose name paid for what pew or stained-glass window. People care about those things. I believe the Spirit is more concerned about the children whose tears have gone unnoticed, whose cries have gone unheeded and unheard. She is more concerned about the abuse running rampant through communities of faith and covered up. More than any place of worship we build, Source is more concerned with the lives of battered women and children silently seated in sanctuaries and synagogues under a ministry that enables their abusers.

The answer, the solution to the problems of domestic violence is, unfortunately, not in the house. There is little, if any, teaching on domestic violence in communities of faith even though one in three women and one in five men will experience this devastation. Most places of worship do not offer support or resources for abuse victims. There is rarely teaching or training on how to handle the problem many times because leaders are not open to scrutiny of their own abuse, or they don't want to involve social services. It is a point of pride to be able to do it all so rather than collaborate with agencies that could help, they discourage outside help or ignore the problem altogether claiming, "not in my church." Thus, the problem is not even discussed, especially over the pulpit with the exception of a stay and pray or leave but cleave message.

We are the tabernacle of God. We are his workmanship created in his image with the power to heal, to restore, to recover. We are the hand and heart of God in the earth, pre-ordained to build one another up and give life. We are the people others are seeking for answers, love, wisdom, non-judgement, and a listening ear. It's not in the house! It's in us. Or is it?

Little Gods

Now when the people saw that Moses was delayed coming down from the mountain, the people gathered together to Aaron, and said to him, "Come, make us gods that shall go before us; for as for this Moses, the man who brought us up out of the land of Egypt, we do not know what has become of him." – Exodus 32:1 (KJV)

Many of us suffer from golden calf syndrome. We surrender our personal power and worship false gods. Whenever we give someone control over our lives, our choices, our emotions, our associations, where and how we live, move, and have our being, we make them little gods.

The Israelites got tired of waiting for Moses, God's man who had led them out of captivity. He was not coming down from the mountain fast enough for them. In fear, they turned to the familiar. Their old masters in Egypt had worshipped at the altar of the golden calf Api. Because the people's faith was weak, their patience short, and their thinking dominated by fear, they returned to what they had seen and known, bowing down, and worshipping an idol they set up and sacrificed themselves on.

We cannot condemn the Israelites. We do the same thing. When we are afraid, when we are seeking acceptance, when things get harder than we expected, we re-attach ourselves to our bondage because it is familiar ground and at least we know what to expect. We become like dogs returning to our own vomit. "Better the devil you know than the devil you don't." Unfamiliar terrain is strange and frightening, especially if it means traversing dangerous territory that will change you and your family's entire lives.

The Israelites saw the smoke and heard the thunder rumbling atop that mountain. My guess is they supposed their leader was dead and had left them deserted in the wilderness. The wilderness is a rough and rugged place, full of vipers and unknown elements. These people felt lost, abandoned, and terrified. I know that feeling.

In my own wilderness experiences, I have felt deserted. More than once, I sought out something familiar to fall back on. I thought about going back because I didn't know what was ahead and from where I stood at that moment, it didn't look good. I rationalized the abusive behavior I had become accustomed to. When I was being abused but my children were not, I rationalized the children's need for stability when, in reality, any child who witnesses physical, emotional, financial, or psychological abuse suffers from de facto abuse. The two things playing in that child's mind are how can I protect my parent and will I be next?

We find reasons to stay, to delay. We return to relationships that have shown no evidence of lasting change. We create fantasies around what we want that does not exist in real time. We lie to ourselves even as we struggle to believe the lie. We surrender to unhealthy friendships that smack of the same violations of the spirit and soul that we left. We make sex, drugs, alcohol, people pleasing, work, and other escape hatches our little gods. Anything is better than feeling abandoned, hopeless, and helpless.

The problem with little gods is they have little power. God, Allah, Jehovah, Yahweh, Source Energy, Universal Intelligence, whatever name, if any, you want to give that higher power, has already endowed us with supernatural energy and might. We have been given authority, all power in heaven and earth, power to tread and crush the serpents and scorpions, the fears, bad memories, circumstances that stick their heads up and present their stingers to poison our attitudes and destroy us from without and within.

It may take time to realize, accept, and walk in the authority given us by

Source. It is only when we recognize our power that we can accept the possibility of absolute freedom. We can learn to live an abundant life no matter the present circumstance. As we move forward, we too can reach our promised land, or at least get pretty damned close.

Religion – vs – Relationship

Religion is not man's relationship to God; it is man's relationship to man. – Elie Wiesel

Spirituality is a personal relationship with the Divine. Religion is crowd control. – *Unknown*

In my lifetime I've known many religious folks that have lots of rules, but no genuine lasting relationships. They are "so heavenly high, they are no earthly good." To me, that is what religious folk are all about. They can quote scripture, chapter and verse, Greek and Hebrew translation, breaking down the meaning of every syllable in every line, shooting out doctrine faster than a gunslinger in an old western movie. They dress up for the divine in an effort to impress him, fully clothed in masks that testalie and prophelie till Jesus comes. They say things "in love" with a dagger on their tongue aimed straight for your heart. They debate, judge, scrutinize, challenging you to go public with your sin while keeping their skeletons stuffed to overflow in the back of their closets.

The spirit of religion is foolishness to the divine. The concept of religion did not exist in any language or culture until the 16th and 17th centuries. Yes, people believed in higher powers, spirits and spirit beings, the connection between nature, human beings, and higher life forms. The advent of religion came about with writing and with it rules and regulations to govern human life and animal sacrifice.

I do not know chapter and verse, but the Bible does say that true religion is to visit the sick, take care of the widow (which includes the divorced but that is a subject for another time), and help those in need. Sounds like compassion, kindness, and love to me. If we are truly doing this without ulterior motives, then we can lay honest claim to our spirituality.

Religious folks have so many rules it affects their relationships. I am not against boundaries. I am against bondage and sabotage. Abused women in communities of faith tend to stay in those relationships much longer and with more severe consequences because of religious rules, doctrine, and traditions. It is tradition that binds them to a piece of paper, a ceremony, and a ring. It is doctrine that tells these same women, "God hates divorce," without filling in the blank spaces as to why. Abused women in religious communities often find themselves wrestling with religious rules and regulations which say that they will lose God's love, incur his wrath, be guilty of sin, and doomed to hell if they leave and/or divorce their husbands. Women are not often, if at all, given the full revelation of scripture which reveals that God hated how women were treated in divorce proceedings. They were cast out with nothing. They were left unprotected, impoverished, abandoned, and alone. Women were forced into prostitution to feed themselves and their children who were thrown out with them. God hated the evil men did to the women they divorced. God is not angry when cutting the cord is necessary to preserve life, including mental health. A religion that makes marriage sacrosanct at the cost of life is not biblically correct, loving, or sanctioned by God.

I do believe religion has a place as a foundation for good. A religion, however, that keeps women and children powerless, subservient, uneducated, abused, voiceless, and without honor, is not in line with what the creator purposed for the created. In the beginning, God looked at all he created and said, "That's good." (Genesis 1:31a) If we are to believe what this word says then we must recognize that what God denoted as good was not gender specific. Not sexual orientation specific. Not race specific. Not culturally specific. Not religiously specific. It was all good.

Religion will have you believing that God asks us to sacrifice all of our gifts, talents, skills, and abilities without seeking compensation when the Bible clearly states, "the workman is worthy of his hire." (Luke 10:7b) Religion will try to convince you that poverty is a blessing, a badge of honor to be worn with pride when scripture actually says, "I wish above all things that you would prosper and be in good health, even as thy soul prospers. (3rd John 2)." The will of the Divine is that we be well rounded, living abundantly in all areas of our lives.

This type of religion could cost you your life and your livelihood. A mentor of mine once told me, "God is not on welfare. He pays for what he asks for." Your source is not a reverse Robin Hood, stealing from the poor and giving imbalanced offerings to church leadership. The creator is balanced in everything. There are four seasons – winter, spring, summer, fall. Each one balances the other. There is night for rest and day for work. There is life which balances death and vice versa.

It is impossible for religious folks to have real relationships when they are not real. They wear Dunbar's mask that "grins and lies." This charade demands that you not talk about your problems or great escapes. Do not enjoy your love and certainly not your love making. Be more conscious of demonic spirits than God conscious. Flee everything! Live for heaven or burn in hell but whatever you do, do not enjoy your life here on earth right now. Admitting truth, being real, yanking off the covers and exposing the charade could blow a religious community apart. What would remain if that ever happened?

Jesus, the expert teacher, expounded so often on truth and love, yet the religious folks of his day missed it every time. The more enlightenment Jesus shared, the more afraid the religious community became. Jesus was messing up their control and hindering their collection plate. Jesus repeatedly said, "God is love." The religious practice then was to buy that love with offerings to the church. Jesus said again, "You will know them by their love. (John 13:35)." He proclaimed those who can genuinely love will not be recognized by their sect, religious organization, or family lineage. They will come in all shapes, forms, size, sexes, and cultures. You will not be able to tell who they are by their garb, the color of their skin, their religious or political affiliation. You will only be able to distinguish them by their love, how they treat one another and all of humanity. Jesus' teachings about money, love, and relationship, exposed the true identity of many of the religious leadership as thieves, thugs, and liars. Needless to say, they were not happy.

Religious communities today have become much like the Pharisees and Sadducees of old who lobbied for Jesus' death and the death and torture of anyone who went against them. The church was the political power of the day that connected with the political powers of Rome. The decision to kill Jesus was both a political and financial one.

Many people who have told the truth about their abuse in communities of faith, especially at the hands of religious leadership, have been ostracized and excommunicated. Their perpetrators and leaders elevated and protected. A Catholic nun in India, raped 13 times by her bishop, was pressured into keeping silent. If it were not for the cadre of sisters that stood with her, she may not have had the courage to stand up for herself (Abi-Habib & Raj, 2019). A pastor who tied his wife to their bed, beat, and raped her then got himself ready to go and preach, testified in court that he had at least loosened the ropes at her request.

In his mind, that was an act of kindness. His wife had escaped and, naked, ran to a neighbor's house for help. The pastor's congregation strongly supported him during the trial based on the verse, "Touch not God's anointed and do his servant no harm."

While doing my research on domestic abuse and violence in faith communities, I came across the story of a young woman who was a member of the congregation of a famous minister who was also a best-selling author. When she left her abusive husband, she and her children were ostracized and ignored because she refused to be quiet about her husband's abuse. Her husband was in a leadership position in the church.

Then there is my own story. My own experience. Much of the church counsel I sought blamed me and ignored my voice and the voices of my two oldest children who confronted youth leaders about the abuse in our family. I was told by my pastor to keep the house clean, keep the children clean and quiet, have dinner on the table when my husband got home from work, and to make sure his needs were met. In other words, if I were submissive and a good wife, things would change. In my mind, the message was, "it's your fault. If you change, he will change." I was being held responsible for my husband's behavior.

I was so confused and hurt. I had always taken care of my family and several times heard him take the credit. My teenaged children were also confused. They had sought help and found none. We felt like no one was listening. No one cared. I believed my husband when he said, "People know how you are." How was I? My husband convinced me that I was a drama queen and people knew it. So, I kept silent.

My husband was partially correct. There were people who knew me. They also recognized the signs and symptoms of abuse. Two such sisters in the church reached out to me. Two of the brothers reached out to correct my husband. Even though I did not readily avail myself of their help, it encouraged me to know that someone saw, and someone cared.

There are many voices crying out in the wilderness of sanctuaries, synagogues, and mosques. Pressured by those in spiritual authority, by traditions of men, and doctrine of elders, they are told to be quiet, to serve, to remain, and God will bless them and their marriage, so they stay. Conflicted by what they have believed about God and what people of God have shown them or done to them, they remain bound by the doctrine of the submissive.

A friend of mine once spoke truth to me that pierced my heart. After listening to my long diatribe about things happening at my church, he asked me who I worship. I didn't understand and of course answered, God. He asked me if I was sure. I was offended. Of course I was sure. He said, often we think we are worshipping God when, in fact, we are worshipping a pastor or the person in leadership. He asked me again if I know who I worship. I did not answer. I realized then that I had given worship to a false God. I was loathe to admit that.

Religion did not exist in the beginning of time. It was developed over hundreds of years by people attempting to achieve power over others. Relationship to others and all living things, trees, forests, the sun, moon, and stars, the seas and sky, heaven and earth, existed before time began. It is the relationship to your source that empowers the relationship you have with yourself and others. Religion does not a relationship make.

Until we stop making untouchable gods of those in spiritual authority, we cannot see God as he really is. Until we stop advocating for instead of against abuse because of the cloth someone is wearing, we will not be able to see the divinity in ourselves. Until we remove the mask, take the blinders off, and tell the truth, we will never be able to free ourselves or anyone else from the false doctrine and beliefs that imprison us all. Until we get real, we cannot get right. Our lives can't get right. Our relationships can't get right. Our family, our communities, our country, the world can't get right as long as we continue to live the lie, putting on more and more false faces until, eventually, we smother ourselves to death.

A Prayer of Deliverance

Lord, I know I've done the right thing,
Now give me the strength to do the rest.
Empower me to do what it takes to right myself
To free myself from the snares of the enemy in the inner me
Let the words of my mouth
And the meditations of my heart,

> The things I speak,
> The things I think about
> The things I desire

Be acceptable in the light of your vision for my life
You, O God, the source of all that is, was and is to come

> Be my safe place
> My fortress
> My strong tower
> My strength
> My deliverance
> My invisible shield
> My redeemer

So that I may redeem my soul from pain, anguish, and fear

> My spirit from discouragement, discontent, and doubt

Speak to me in the night times
Cause me to hear your loving kindness in the morning
Help me to stay focused on the goal.
What is the goal?

> Freedom
> Freedom for myself to fully be myself
> Freedom for my children
> For my ancestors and descendants
> Freedom for my generations from the bondage of abuse and

betrayal.
I cast off every spirit of oppression and depression.

Every spirit of fear, intimidation, rejection, and humiliation.
By my word
I bring to nothing every destructive word or deed
Past, present, and future.
I go free now and forever
In the omnipotent power of God,
My source
That now works and operates freely and fully within me.
I have been transferred and transformed
Delivered from the kingdom of darkness
Into the kingdom of glorious light
Incredible illumination
Wherein I was blind
Now I can see with acute precision
And focused vision.
I love you
I thank you
I give you gratitude daily
For wisdom, knowledge and understanding
For leading me and guiding me into all truth
Thank you most of all for loving me unconditionally
I commit to love myself the same
Thank you for always causing me to triumph
Amen
Selah
It is so
And so it is!

First Love – A Prayer

Dear God
Who loves me
Across that crowded space
Of time and eternity
Do you see me?

Dear God
Who loves me
Understanding my thoughts afar off
And those feelings I can only express
In tears and groanings
Whose thoughts are higher than mine
Who alone knows the thoughts
And intents
Of my heart
Speak to me.

Dear God
Who loves me
When I yearn so deeply
For a special touch
For affection and attention
So much that it becomes a physical hurt
Bathe me in your presence
Replenish my spirit
So that I may live.
Cause me to hear your loving kindness in the morning
And your sweet song at night
Be my Jehovah Ishi
Who provides all warmth
            And comfort
            For me.

Dear God
Who loves me
Be my God

My source,
My protector,
My friend
Amen

4 *CHAPTER FOUR*

<u>The Bent Over Woman</u>

And behold, there was a woman which had a spirit of infirmity eighteen years, and was bowed together (bent double), and could in no wise lift herself up. — Luke 13:11 (KJV)

When I was 29 years young, I attended a *Super Cupboard* given by the Catholic Sisters of the Bernadine in Chester, PA. I was a single mom struggling with feeding my two children and keeping a roof over our heads after my first husband and I separated. The sisters helped the four families attending this meeting with food, information, and resources. There was a young lady, we'll call her Diana, about 24 years old who attended with her two children, ages three and four, who looked like twins. The three year old was inquisitive and restless, always moving, always doing something. The four-year-old was stoic, unusually quiet, and very mature. At the end of the Super Cupboard, the sisters asked us to reflect on the scripture in Luke 13:11 concerning the bent over woman and write down our thoughts. As I did so, I thought of Diana and her children.

Diana was about five feet three inches tall and couldn't have weighed more than 100 pounds soaking wet. She looked tired. At only 24, life seemed to have bested her. She was angry, fearful, and frustrated. She lived in a temporary housing facility. Donations of food, clothing, furniture, and household appliances came into the shelter daily for the express purpose of helping those in need get back on their feet. Facility employees often stole these donations. Diana and others had witnessed the thefts and, as a result, were threatened with a call to children and youth services and having their children taken away if they told anyone. This practice is common in homeless shelters.

As Diana told of the threat of losing her children, she broke into a flood of tears. Homelessness was humiliating enough without the threats. Diana recalled all the promises of help that never came. The limited time she had to live at the facility. The fear of not knowing what to do or where to go next. I was only four years older than Diana. As I listened to her speak, I became outraged at man's inhumanity to man. All of us in the room had been bent over by life's circumstances. I was angry for all the woman like Diana, like me, like the other women in the room who met with struggle from sunrise to sunset. Whose backs were bent, and hearts broken by burdens they carried year after tedious year. Who looked for help only to find judgement, turned up noses, scorn, and threats. It was not enough that Diana felt she had been brought to a place where she had almost no control over her life and the lives of her children. She had also become a pawn in a chess game of power and control in a place where she thought she and her children would be safe.

In the story of the bent over woman, Jesus was teaching in one of the synagogues when he saw her. This woman had been crippled, bent, and bowed, for eighteen years. As a result, she was labeled an outcast from society. People wouldn't talk to her or touch her. Instead, she was treated as though she were diseased and invisible.

Years ago, a date and I, we'll call him Chris, decided to walk a little after eating a big fancy meal at a jazz club. I couldn't eat all of my food, so I had a carryout portion left. As we walked along, I noticed a young man sitting dejected against a brick wall. There were people milling all around as this was a high traffic area with movie and club goers everywhere. No one noticed this young man. He looked exhausted, hungry, and hopeless. I asked Chris, to go over and give my warm carry-out food to the young man. Chris looked at me as if I had lost my mind, but he honored my request. The young man looked shocked and relieved when Chris tapped his shoulder and handed him the food. Together, we told the young man, God bless you. He nodded his head, opened up the box and began eating. Chris and I continued to the parking lot. Chris was visibly shaken by the expression on the young man's face. I explained to him that everyone wants to be acknowledged. That all the people milling around that man pretended not to see him. His situation was glaringly evident, but it is easier to look away. To everyone else, that young man had become invisible.

I don't know what happened to that young man, but I know that day, that moment, someone saw him, someone touched him, and someone met a need. I know that day he felt seen just as the bent over woman must have felt when Jesus took notice of her from the distance.

How often do we walk by the homeless and pretend not to see them? According to the National Network to End Domestic Violence, up to 57% of homelessness among women and children is caused by domestic violence (National Network to End Domestic Violence, 2018). How often have we judged the lives of abused women and said things like, "that couldn't/wouldn't be me" and "there ain't that much love in the world." When have we ever intervened to rescue a child or to make a safe space for him or her to be? What has been our contribution to the solution?

Jesus saw the bent over woman. He immediately identified what had brought her so low she could only see things at ground level. It wasn't something she had done wrong. It wasn't a health issue. It wasn't her fault. Jesus had compassion for her. He knew her infirmity was not caused by sins she or her parents had committed, a common theme in his day. The Bible says that she was bent over by a spirit.

Quite often when we think of spirits, we think of spiritual beings, but there are things that damage your spirit causing you to be bent and broken. Homelessness comes with a spirit of humiliation, hopelessness, and fear. Sexual assault and abuse come with a polluted spirit of shame, guilt, and unworthiness. Psychological abuse comes with a spirit of fear, apprehension, anxiety, depression, and post-traumatic stress disorder. Suffering has side effects. Grief will bend your spirit over. What happens in the spiritual will often begin exhibiting itself in the natural. Jesus saw everything that had bent this woman over. He identified what had brought her so low, what had her bent and bowed. He did not judge her or ignore her. He saw her.

Jesus could have chosen to meet this woman outside after services and talk to her privately. Instead, he reached out and called her to him publicly. He knew he could help her and heal her. He showed the crowd gathered there, that there was nothing to be afraid of. That she was not untouchable or unclean.

We tend to place value on people according to their condition, place, income, age, or appearance. The bent over woman was treated as less than because she could not stand up. Because she could not stand up, she could not look up. She was isolated because she had no vision for herself or her future. She was condemned because folks believed her condition had been caused by her sin, by something she had done wrong. They ignored the fact that, though she had the condition for 18 years, there was a time when she was standing tall. The Bible does not say she had the condition her entire life, but 18 years of it. What laid her low, crouching at the pedestal of hell? Jesus saw it all, and he called her to him with the express purpose of freeing her from other's judgements and healing her spirit from what had caused her deformity.

Jesus spoke a word of healing over the woman. He spoke to her spirit. He spoke to her soul. He spoke a word and released her from the wounds and words of the past that had crippled her. All the negative words that had been spoken over and about her were nullified and voided. He spoke hope and life to her. Her imprisonment was broken, and she was set free to see a bigger and better vision for her life. Then he touched her, a forbidden gesture, and immediately she stood up straight.

Words are powerful. Psychological and emotional abuse are the forerunners of physical abuse and the most insidious. The abuser uses words to consign their victims to a prison without walls, cells, or bars. Gaslighting is a poison that paralyzes its victims, the venom remaining in the body and mind for years or a lifetime. The secrets that we don't say, the horrors that we don't tell turn on us, the stress of it causing our bodies to fight against itself physically and mentally. And as we carry these burdens, we begin to lean over in spirit until we are so bent and bowed, we are unable, incapable of looking up from the ground. We accept this position as our lot, as our curse, as our fault.

Jesus released the bent over woman with a fresh word. He spoke death to the thing that caused her suffering and life to a new beginning. Before he touched her with his hands, his word had already done the thing whereto he had sent it. Her standing up was the result of the word she received and the faith she had in that word to accomplish its end. When she stood, she got a new vision. She could see something better for her life. Imagine being bent over, only seeing dirt and stone, people's feet rushing about, enduring pain day-after-day, hearing the gossip about you all around you. When she stood up, she could see the sky and trees, feel the wind gently touch her face instead of howling at her back. When she stood up, because she was able to see things differently, she could dream a new dream. She saw hope and her perspective was immediately changed. She rejoiced and the crowd who had judged and rejected her, rejoiced with her.

Women who experience domestic violence and abuse are bent over in humility, fear, depression, anger, physical and emotional pain, and grief. They need someone to see them without judging. To identify what has brought them so low. To not close their eyes because the sight of them is too hard to deal with. An abused woman is a bent over woman. Bent over from sorrow. Bent over from helplessness. Bent over from hopelessness. They may look like the businessperson in an elegant suit or expensive shoes with red bottoms. They may look like the homemaker who comes to church with perfect children and a ready smile. They may look like the homeless woman roaming the street and talking to herself because she has lost herself and her mind. They may look like you. They may look like me. They may need you to speak a word to them. A word of healing. A word of hope. One word that may change their lives forever.

When Jesus spoke to the bent over woman he said, "Woman, you are set free from your infirmity." He said it before it happened. He said it as she was still leaning over. He said it in faith and the woman received his words in faith. This woman could have refused to come forward. She could have been afraid because of the crowd. But she came willingly. She reached for the help that was offered. She had faith in his words, the words of a stranger. His touch was one of confident reassurance. Because he wasn't afraid, neither was she. Because he was confident, it emboldened her. By faith, she stood up and began her life anew.

There is another side to the story. When you get your healing, when you become free, everybody is not going to be happy about it, especially those who aided and abetted your bondage. Jesus did not deliver the woman in an enclosed area. What he did, he did publicly, shaming the religious leaders of the day. The synagogue ruler was outraged, incensed, indignant. Jesus had taken over the services and healed this woman publicly, on the sabbath, in the sanctuary, with so great a crowd of witnesses that Jesus' power and authority over the situation was undeniable. The synagogue leader felt insulted, embarrassed, and humiliated. How dare this Jesus take over his services! Jesus had, in effect, defied the synagogue leader's authority. This leader was quick to spew venom at the cheering crowd in the form of scripture. "There are six days in which men ought to work: in them therefore come and be healed, and not on the sabbath day" (Luke 13:14).

The leader did not speak to Jesus or the woman, but to the crowd. In order to maintain his power and control over the masses, he attempted to gaslight the public by openly chastising Jesus and the woman, placing them in the roles of lawbreaker and sinner.

Many women are involved in a toxic religion that demands they stay and pray. When they contest this kind of thinking, the same age-old doctrine that we saw in the patria protesta, they are often met with scripture used to keep them oppressed, confused, and submissive. This tactic is as old as religious time.

Jesus called this leader and his cronies, hypocrites. The word sabbath means rest and liberation. Jesus gave the woman rest from her crippling burden. He liberated her from the bondage of her infirmity. The synagogue leader knew the meaning of the word sabbath. The man's devotion was to the study of the law and its words. He did not want the people to know what he knew. Jesus took him and the other leaders to task for trying to deceive the people. He chastised them by saying you even let your oxen out to rest on the sabbath, should I then not give this woman rest from her indignities? To add insult to injury, Jesus said, she is a child of Abraham too, and thus an heir in the blessing. This may have caused the crowd to question the authority of the synagogue's leadership. What else had they been telling them that wasn't quite what the scriptures really said?

The methodology of psychological and emotional abuse is to get the victim to believe a lie by mixing it with half-truths, thus causing the victim to question their own reality. Jesus condemned this at the highest levels. His honesty, openness, and ability to sway the crowds was messing with the financial affairs, power, and authority of these toxic leaders. Though there were some spiritual leaders who did align themselves with Jesus' teachings, those whose egos Jesus had bruised, eventually petitioned the government to have Jesus tortured and crucified on the pretense of treason to the state. Crucifixion was the punishment for criminals. Jesus was tried, found guiltless, and still crucified. The Roman leaders had egos to protect too.

I have no doubt Jesus could have healed the bent over woman from where she stood. Instead, he called her to him. Called her out of the crowd just as he did the woman with the issue of blood. He wanted other people to see her as he saw her. Not as a crippled woman, but as an empowered woman standing strong. This is what the sisters of the Bernardine did for us during and after the Super Cupboard. They not only gave us all fish; they taught us new ways of fishing and how to multiply what we had. More importantly, they never let go. Their mission was to help us stand back up on our own, to see ourselves as Jesus saw us, empowered and strong.

As to Diana, I never saw or heard from her again, even though I gave her my number and asked her to keep in touch if she needed anything. The sisters of the Bernardine also reached out to her, and to all of us long after the Super Cupboard was over. I prayed then that God would give me wisdom to write with such power that thousands of Diana's are touched, redeemed, and healed through the words; that ignorance of human conditions is given light; and bent over women whose backs carry years of bondage are immediately made straight. I imagined then churches and communities collaborating to empower women in poverty, bent over by sickness, systemic racism, classism, abuse, injustice.

More than three decades after drafting the original article about the bent over woman, I am still challenging myself to be like Jesus, calling out injustice and ignorance. Speaking to women bent by life. Offering hope and help. Empowering women to stand. While writing and editing this book, I wrestled with the question of, what if what I say hurts or hinders rather than helps someone. What if I say something wrong or damaging? What if I do more harm than good? I stopped writing many times because I was afraid that my words might do damage in someone's life. I knew the importance of words and had experienced the damage they could cause. I was still wrestling with the value of my own voice, my own words until a person I respect and admire said, "Write the words. Finish the book. Even if only one person is helped, that's one life where you've made a difference."

Jesus made a difference one life at a time. I challenge you to do the same. If you can be a safe place, offer a safe space for a woman or a child in need of rescue, you can change the trajectory of generations one life at a time. You don't have to feed 5,000. If you have fed, clothed, sheltered just one, you have potentially changed 10,000 lives. If you can speak or write a few words that give hope to someone bowed in submission to abuse and domestic violence, you have carried on the work of Spirit, the work of Christ. If you have been or are currently being abused and can draw up enough courage to reach out for help, if you have faith the size of a miniscule mustard seed, then perhaps you too can arise from the bent over position and see a new day dawning for yourself and those you love. Selah and amen.

Wonder Women

A woman who can move on his invincible. – T. D. Jakes

After coming out of its cocoon, the butterfly never crawls along the ground as in the caterpillar state. No matter what anybody says, wants, or even demands, that butterfly cannot and will not ever go back to what it was before it got its wings.

One of the most difficult things about leaving an abusive relationship is keeping focused on the forward motion as opposed to doing the backstroke. Moving forward is a continual process and is often heart wrenching, emotional and physical work.

There is the work of renewing your mind. Reminding yourself of who you are, who you were created to be and understanding that you are worthy of love, peace, and joy. This is the work of breaking old contracts with yourself that say you are unworthy, unlovable, and unfixable. There is the work of rebuilding, reconstructing your life, and quite possibly your children's lives. That may mean moving to another city or state, starting over in a new home or unfamiliar environment, leaving one job or one church for another. There is the physical and psychological makeover which may involve a long stretch of rehabilitation and therapy. There is the work of loving yourself again which includes facing the truth about your relationship and the lies you've told yourself in order to get through it. The justifications you've told others in order to live behind the curtain and not expose your spouse, your lover, your best friend, your relative, your pastor or church leader. There is the strengthening of the heart and soul in order to get through the crushing heartbreak of it all.

If you are blessed, that means empowered, to finish all of this work, then there follows the work of forgiving yourself and putting your hands to the plow without looking back. It takes focus, a great deal of support, and a tremendous amount of energy not to turn around. Let's be clear about that.

If the butterfly were to crawl back into the cocoon, he would surely die. The butterfly was always destined to fly. When we go back to our former lives, our former selves, we lose ourselves. The more we return to what was, the more of ourselves and our families we put at risk. It is only in moving forward, changing the narrative, setting the boundaries, taking the leap that we may gain any sense of renewal, balance, stability, peace, and order in our lives even though those first steps and falls may seem pretty shaky.

We are marvelous creatures, as magnificent in beauty and wonder as the butterfly. We were crafted in darkness by the hand of an unseen power far greater than ourselves. Every cell was calculated and distributed, every neuron, proton, atom, axon, and dendrite placed specifically for its function. Endowed with all the universe has to offer, we are strengthened. We can go on.

Captured

I looked at the net and struggled in it, tangling myself all up. I didn't realize the net was for safety, not capture. — K. J. Sharpe

I admit. I am not as trusting as I used to be. I had a propensity to look for the good in everybody and everything. My children said to me, "Mom, you're just too trusting" and "You mother everybody."

My trusting nature took blow after blow for literal decades before I came to a place of trusting no one and analyzing the motives of even the kindest, most devoutly sincere people. So, it came to be, that I struggled with asking and allowing people to help me.

Have you ever heard the story of the man who drowned in a flood waiting for God to save him? As the story goes, the man is offered help many times. First by a driver who offers to take him to safety when the rains begin. Second by a man in a boat who offers to take him to safety when the flood water is at the man's doorstep and in his living room. Third, and finally, by a helicopter pilot when flood waters have engulfed the man's house to the point where he is left standing on his roof. The man dismisses every offer with, "No. God will save me."

The man drowns, dies, then stands before God angry and complaining. "I believed in you. Why didn't you save me?" God reminds the man of all the help he refused. He assures the man that he was never forsaken but that he had refused help, safety, and protection.

There are times when we are like that man. When people try to help us, we let our pride and fear get in the way. We are suspicious and struggle fearing the net set out to catch us is for capture or imprisonment. If you have been in an abusive relationship, you learn that a smile, a kind word, and I love you, cannot always be trusted.

It is not a sin or a shame to be fearful or lacking in faith. Don't beat yourself up about that. Analyzing people and situations is often in your best interest. It is when you over analyze to the point of paralysis, and fear to the point of immobility that you lose ground. It is when your pride gets in the way of your need that you miss the mark.

Move with wisdom. Get help. Get support. Get knowledge. Get understanding. By all means, do your due diligence and when genuine help comes, learn how to recognize it, and do not reject it. Ascertain who is holding the net. It may be the universe capturing you for safety, not imprisonment.

Release

The most painful thing is losing yourself in the process of loving someone too much, and forgetting that you are special too. —Ernest Hemmingway

Turn your wounds into wisdom.-Oprah Winfrey

We have all been neglected, rejected, used, and abused at one time or another in our lives. From the belligerent salesclerk to our calls being transferred from one voice message to another, to the person we love acting like a jerk. We have all had our share of frustration, anger and hurt. Pain is a part of life. We have inflicted it on ourselves and others, often in equal measure to what has been inflicted upon us. We are all guilty of causing and experiencing pain. Nothing comes through this life without it. The real problem occurs when we insist on holding on to our suffering.

I mentored young women for several years. There were a few young ladies who refused to let go of their emotional trauma surrounding fathers who had abandoned them physically and emotionally. These young ladies continually tried to gain their father's love, acceptance, validation, and approval only for their errant dads to come up short every time. It did not matter that the young ladies had family and friends who loved, cared for, and supported them. Even exceptional stepfathers could not compete or compare to the love these girls yearned for from their biological fathers. These young ladies focused so much on what they didn't get from the man whose loins gave them life; they took everyone else for granted. They held on to the pain of rejection to the detriment of themselves, becoming self-centered, self-absorbed, abrasive adults, dragging their sorrow around with them like corpses hanging onto the backs of the living. They blamed and belittled insisting everyone partake of their misery. They and their bitterness were inseparably linked, all because they chose to carry the pain instead of letting it go.

Life can throw some deadly blows. People disappoint us, betray us, and leave us hanging or holding the bag. Abusive relationships can leave us brutally scarred mentally, physically, sexually, emotionally, financially, and psychologically. We can lose the people we love, have our dreams fall apart, be wracked with pain from an incurable disease. Life can hit hard.

There is nothing you can do about what has already happened to you. Even a past that is only minutes behind you is unalterable. You can only live in the moment. You have to release the past. How do you do that? Allow yourself to feel whatever it is you feel. Scream, cry, shout, run, throw things. Whatever it is that you need to do without hurting yourself or someone else, do it. You will need to release those feelings and emotions. You may have to, at least temporarily, draw a line putting up a barrier between the things or people that hurt you, so you don't lose your mind. If that is what it takes to keep you from falling apart, then let that be so. If it means living in a season of sorrow, then let that be so. If it means isolating yourself so you can get a grip and find yourself, then let that be so. But at the end of your mourning, at the end of your sorrow, at the end of your darkness and the lines you have drawn to keep others out and away from an unbearable grief, you will have to find the strength to release it and move on. If you are to survive and thrive, you cannot live among the dead things.

It took over a decade for me to learn that I did not deserve to be abused and mishandled by my husband and the church. I held on to both anger and sorrow for several years. I loved my husband desperately and was highly disappointed that things didn't work out. I had planned to be with this man sitting on our front porch holding hands while we rocked in our rocking chairs and watched our great grandchildren play in the yard. For years I blamed myself for this vanishing dream. I had been married before and failed, thus I saw myself as a failure. I had been told that it was my fault. That as a woman I should have, could have, must have done something wrong. I believed this for an extended period of time. I could not forgive myself. I could not forgive people who had hurt me, used me, and betrayed me. It took several years to lay aside the guilt, to work on forgiveness, to let go of some things and put it all behind me. I finally recognized that a failed marriage did not mean I am a failure. It meant that I had the courage to open myself up to love again. There is no crime or guilt in that. Neither is there any condemnation in moving on.

No matter what happened to you or how bad it was, it is in your past. You must continue. You are a unique human being. There is no one like you in the world. You were chosen from over two million sperm to be here. You were the strongest, the fastest, the most determined from conception. That is how you got into this earth's realm and that indefatigable strength has not diminished. Do not stop now. Deal with your heartbreaks and heartache. Contend with your disappointments and the disaster that may be your life right now. Allow yourself to feel every bit of your pain but do not build a house and live there. Face the neglect, the rejection, that abuse that tried to obliterate you. Face it down and say enough. You are enough. Deal with the pain of your past. Accept all of it. Everything that tore you apart. If you need to take the fight to court, do it. If you need to fight through it in therapy, don't put that off. Do it now. Scream, cry, and wrestle with the thing if you need to. And after it has all been said and done, after you have done all that can be done, release it and move on.

Notice I said release, not forget. Unless you have a disease that affects your hippocampus, memories never leave. But they can be rendered ineffective.

When my daughter was young, I shared a story with her about a howling dog who sat on a porch next to his master. The dog kept howling and crying while his master rocked leisurely in his chair, smoking on his pipe. A man walking by stopped and asked, "Mister, what's wrong with your dog?" The man said, "Nothing. He's sitting on a nail, but he refuses to get up." The dog had become so accustomed to his pain that he refused to move from it. We can get comfortable in our bondage.

If this season in your life is going to be different, drastically different, you have got to face, allow, and release the pain. You can't pretend it doesn't exist. You have to have the guts to face it and to, at some point, tear your focus from it and live on abundantly. In order to do that, you have to get perspective on your pain. You have to find yourself in all the mixture of additives that conjured up the poison in your life. You have to break agreements that you've made against yourself to hinder your forward movement. Get help when and where you need it to release the past and the pain.

Affirmation – I Accept

I accept that I am love, lovable, and lovely.

>After all

>I was created to be so

>>Therefore

>>>I accept.

I accept that I am power full.

>Not power less

>The above only

>And not the beneath

>The head

>>With direction and vision

>Not the tail

>>That blindly follows.

I am the doorway.

>Not the door mat

I open myself to the responsibility of being me.

>Loving me, flaws and all

I accept the challenge of being me.

>Yes

I accept who I am as I am.

I accept that I am perfectly imperfect without and within

The strength of my source operating within me

>   Perfects my weaknesses

>   Therefore,

>   I accept all that I am,

>   And the perfection of my source

>   In the absence of my own

I accept that I do not now have or need all the answers.

I accept that the answers will be given to me as I need them.

>   When I am ready to receive them

>   In the right moment

>   And at the perfect time

>   I accept.

I accept that I am a student of the universe.

I accept that I am learning.

>   I am learning to be patient.

>   I am learning to be still and know.

>   I am learning to meditate and wait.

In all my learning I am receiving wisdom, knowledge, and

Above all

Understanding, compassion for myself and others,

and truth.

I accept this elevation and education.

I accept that in order to fulfill the visions and dreams set before me

There is a process.

I accept the process.

I accept that I am finite,

And my source and love are infinite and eternal.

I accept that all things are working together for my good,

No matter how bad it looks.

All things are creating the beautiful tapestry that is my life.

Nothing

If I allow it

Is ever wasted.

I accept that the universe will make everything perfect

Supreme

Sublime

In its time

    I accept.

I accept that I am worthy of love, wealth, health, riches, honor, and long life.

I accept that these things are given to me by divine right.

I accept that I deserve and am responsible for my own happiness.

    With joy and exuberance

    Fully matured

    I accept and claim the inheritance of peace that I know is mine.

And so it is.

Selah and Amen.

I accept.

5 *CHAPTER FIVE*

Living with the Ancients [An Excerpt, (c) 2022, K. J. Sharpe]

We are not makers of history. We are made by history.- Reverend Dr. Martin Luther King Jr.

I have always enjoyed history, especially the study of ancient civilizations. As a teenager, I was fascinated with the study of Egypt. I read about the beautiful, shrewd, black businesswoman and warrior Queen Cleopatra fighting for Egypt, braving battle in hand-to-hand combat alongside Marc Antony. Queen Hatshepsut reigned in Egypt's 18th dynasty for 21 years. Ethiopia's Nubian Queen Candace, the warrior queen, terrified Alexander the Great with her prowess, skill, and command of her male and female troops. Her mother and grandmother were also warrior queens.

Ancient Egyptian women had more rights than any other women in their time. They were seen as persons in their own right, able to defend themselves and bring cases to court, be witnesses in court, file for divorce, own and sell property, write contracts, sue, and be sued, own land, and have their own financial wealth and legacies. Although formal education was forbidden for most Egyptian women, those born to royal households were often educated and could become pharaohs, as in the case of Cleopatra. Unlike Egyptian woman, women's rights in other cultures and countries, including the United States, concerning finance, family, land, and legacy were forbidden up to as late as the 1950's.

Early Greeks and Romans were particularly renowned for their misogynistic treatment of women. Semonides of Amorgos, a popular Greek poet and author, wrote "the worst pestilence Zeus ever made is woman"(Wagner, 2019). Aristotle not only called the female body the "deformity" of man but questioned a woman's value as a sexual partner. Socrates, the Greek philosopher, and Aristotle's teacher identified women as the "weaker sex" (Cole et al., 2005/2012).

Much of the violence against women and children was codified into law. The Romans were strong proponents of the Patria Protesta, the law of fatherly power which gave a father or husband the right as "head of household" to do whatever he willed concerning his spouse, children, and slaves. No matter his status in society, a father or husband had the legal right to abuse, mistreat, maim, torture, or kill his wife and children with impunity. They were his property to do with as he pleased including selling them or marrying them off to pay his debts. A female child was only given the right to live if the father gave his nod of approval. Otherwise, she could be taken up into the mountains and left there to be eaten by animals or starve to death.

The head of household status was transferable to brothers, uncles, and sons. The term "head of household" is still used today as a term denoting women as inferior and needing the "headship" of a man to gain respectability and credibility. Single women of a certain age are still patronized and pressured to get married and have children. They are considered incomplete without a man or a child. Women in parts of Africa, Asia, India, Europe, and the United States are not encouraged or allowed to get an education. Women are still discouraged from studying the sciences, technology, engineering, and mathematics. Two thousand years later, we are still living with ancient beliefs and standards for women.

Before the advent of Christianity as a religion, women were not only close followers of Jesus, but were also prophets, had power and a voice in structure and governance of the movement, were martyrs, and had gospels ascribed to them. Jesus delivered women to be themselves, full partners in his teaching and ministry. He practiced human rights. But when Christianity was adopted by the Roman empire, becoming a legal religion under Constantine, aligned with Rome's patriarchal system, and assimilated with other Roman cults and religions that practiced paternal power, women were stripped of all authority and forced to take a silent seat way in the back. Christian leaders were given power and authority in the Roman Empire and "within three generations, Christianity had gone from being a persecuted faith to a persecuting religion" (Cole et al., 2005/2012, pg 147) .

In the Jewish tradition, the Talmud mentions Lillith as Adam's first wife. Lillith was made at the same time as Adam which made her equal to him. Her role was to submit to him as a help-meet. She chose instead to walk in her authority and power as an equal and thus became a demonic spirit who sucked the life out of men and children. The narrative is that not only were women sinners who threw the world into chaos with their power to seduce, they were also the original progenitors of evil in the world. This narrative was widely read and accepted.

In Greek mythology, Pandora was the errant woman who released all the evils into the world. In Christianity, Eve was the woman who caused man to sin bringing death and destruction to the world. In any and every case, women were portrayed as evil, conniving, untrustworthy, lustful, grasping, greedy, whores, adulterers, unfit, unlovable, unacceptable rejects. This is the legacy of the ancients.

Religion and government were massively intertwined. The high priest was a political appointee. The Pharisees and Sadducees were the two power players in Jewish-Roman history. Zealots were revolutionaries opposed to Roman rule. The Essenes were dismissed by other religious groups. Politics and religion were inseperable.

In the first century A.D. (or C.E.), Saint Jerome, a former monk commissioned by the Damascus Bishop of Rome, translated the New Testament into Latin. The rest he translated later, retaining a great deal of original text from the Greek and Roman traditions. St. Jerome strongly believed women should be neither seen nor heard, especially in the church. His Old and New Testament interpretations became the basis of scripture still largely used today by Catholic and Protestant churches. "Through Christianity, the language, administrative structures, and culture of ancient Rome were preserved and extended" (Cole et al.,2005/2012, pg. 155). This included an extension of some form of the Patria Protesta.

St. Jerome's teachings had a profound effect on later philosophers and spiritual leaders. What this meant for women was the extension of the rules of submissiveness and domesticity as proposed by Aristotle who said, "The relation of male to female is by nature a relation of superior to inferior and ruler to ruled" (Cole et. al,2005/2012, pg. 74). What this has meant for many women in religious communities today is the exploitation of scripture for the purpose of manipulation, gaslighting, and control.

John Piper, a well-known American pastor and author, suggested women endure verbally abusive marriage and "a little smacking around" rather than leave the marriage (Schatz, 2009). In 2013, Pastor Steven J. Cole, suggested a wife "submit" to verbal and emotional abuse and call civil or church authorities if it escalates to physical abuse but she should not divorce her husband. In 2016, actor turned evangelist, Kurt Cameron claimed that "wives are to honor and respect and follow their husband's lead, not to tell their husband how he ought to be a better husband" (Baird & Gleeson, 2018).

Bible scriptures like I Peter 3:1,2; Ephesians 5:22-24; I Timothy 2:11,12; and Colossians 3:18 have all been used to keep women in their place: submissive, subservient, and afraid of God and man. Catholic Bishop Vincent Long, in a 2016 address, cautioned that following purely literal biblical interpretations "provide the basis for systemic oppression or structural discrimination of women and lead communities-even church communities-to protecting perpetrators of domestic violence while simultaneously heaping shame and scorn upon its victims" (Baird & Gleeson, 2018).

Married Christian women and those in other religious communities are one of the most at-risk abused population. Scripture, viewed without the light of history and culture is often used to support a context of abuse. Constrained by cultural beliefs and religious ideologies, women vilified as rebellious, sinful, and un-submissive are twice victimized. When their voices are not heard, their testimonies not given credence, they are forced to re-live the mores and values of ancient male dominated societies. False beliefs concerning a woman's place and value bind women in these communities to a hostage situation, sometimes till death parts them from this life as noted by Julia Baird and Hayley Gleeson: "The past two decades of research has also shown women in religious communities are less likely to leave violent marriages, more likely to believe the abuser will change, less inclined to access community resources and more likely to believe it is their fault; that they have failed as wives as they were not able to stop the abuse" (Baird &

Gleeson, 2018).

Marriage before the 1900's was rarely, if ever, about love and romance. Fathers married off their young girls to secure finances, obtain power, status, land, and to ensure political pacts. Virginity was not about morality or chastity, neither was it necessarily measured by the breaking of the female hymen. It was not required for marriage in ancient Egypt and many other ancient societies. Agrarian fathers devised the concept of virginity as chastity 5,000 to 10,000 years ago as a way to monetize women and girls. It was basically a marketing strategy engineered by the head of households to get the highest bidders for their daughters. Prior to that, definitions of the term were not universal. Virginity could mean proper social behavior, celibacy, or skill in combat depending on what culture and country you came from.

In ancient societies young girls were valued for bearing children that carried on the legacies of the elite. Family members would come and watch the deflowering of a virgin bride. Most of these young brides were between the ages of 14 and 15 with some as young as eight and nine years old. In English common law the age of consent was ten. Early Christianity was infused with myths of 'chaste' women able to fight off demons and cure disease, especially venereal disease, with sex. Virginity tests are still performed on young girls in Afghanistan, Egypt, Iran, Africa, Europe, Asia, Scotland, and parts of the United States. The tale of the virgin cure continues to contribute to a global rape culture among young girls and the disabled (Wagner, 2019).

In Greek society, most young wives were not introduced to their husbands until the "ceremonial transfer of ownership" where the father gave away his daughter with these words: "I give you this girl to plow for the harvesting of children" (Holt, 2016). Today we call this transfer a wedding ceremony.

A common theme in Greek society was, "We have prostitutes [male and female] for pleasure, concubines for daily physical attendance, and wives to bear us legitimate children and to be our faithful housekeepers" (Joshua Cole, et al., 2005/2016, pg. 74). This was the entire goal of marriage. Children carried on legacies, were a source of free labor, were valued investments to buy and sell for profit as slaves and concubines, and to pay off debts. They were financial assets and the man who had his "quiver full" was considered blessed (Psalm 127:4-5). Barren women were considered useless. This belief lasted well into the 1800's.

In the 16th and 17th centuries, bride capture, the practice of raping a woman and then claiming her as your bride, was normal in England. English common law stated, "A husband cannot be guilty of a rape committed by himself upon his lawful wife, for by their mutual matrimonial consent and contract, the wife hath given up herself in this kind to her husband which she cannot retract" (Geis, 1978). It didn't matter that women and young girls were contracted into marriage against their will.

Prosecuting marital rape was unheard of in the United States until the feminist movement of the 1970's. Marital rape wasn't criminalized in the U.S. until 1993, less than 30 years ago. This is attributable to the fact that traditional views of marriage and the cultural, religious, and social mores governing it have not changed much since ancient times.

Black, Native American, and indigenous women of colonized countries were victims of violent rape and exhaustive breeding having no marital rights in the United States, Great Britain, France, the Caribbean islands, and other parts of the world.

Violent sexual assault of indigenous women by European expansionists was a common occurrence, encouraged and sanctioned by law. Christopher Columbus and his crew raped indigenous women frequently and with impunity. In his journal, Columbus wrote of a young native girl whom he called a savage. She fiercely resisted his advances. He dragged her by her hair to his tent, tied her up, and raped her. Afterward, he gleefully reported, "the girl's sexual performance was so satisfying that she might have been trained in a school for whores" (Cole et al., 2005/2012, pg. 281). Neither Columbus nor his peers considered this heinous act savagery or rape. Women and girls who could not protect themselves or speak the language were accused of enflaming the desires of men by their way of dress and their inability to communicate. They were "asking for it."

A pervasive rape culture still exists today because of antiquated belief systems that portray women as property in the case of marriage or kinship, and otherwise inferior beings with seductive evil tendencies that must be subdued. Rape and domestic violence laws in the United States are still not clearly defined or properly adjudicated. In December 2016 Lebanese women protested rape law 522 that gave rapist the right to marry their victims as a way to escape prosecution. It wasn't until August 16, 2017, that the penal code was abolished by parliament. There is no domestic violence legislation in Yemen and no such thing as marital rape in Nigeria. According to the National Network to End Domestic Violence, more than 90% of homeless women experience severe physical and sexual violence at some point in their lives (NNEDV,2018). Murder, rape, and domestic violence suffered by Native American and indigenous women in the United States remains higher than any other race or nationality at a whopping 96% (Wilcox, 2019).

Marriage as a social institution was originally created by Babylonian King Hammurabi of Mesopotamia. Hammurabi liked things in writing. The

Hammurabi codes were written on large black phallic hroughout the kindom. These laws were written on a phallic shaped black stone pillars plaed throughout the kingdom. These laws included requirements for written marriage contracts and divorce papers which had not previously existed. Prior to these written laws, people lived with and had children by whomever they wanted and for however long. When men got tired of their women, they threw them out into the streets with nothing. Women who did not have another male relative to attach herself to, became prey or resorted to prostitution, a legal profession, to survive. In the story of Ruth, Naomi tells her daughter in law that she has no more sons for her to marry. In other words, there is no one else who will cover her. Ruth follows Naomi to the land of her countrymen and marries a cousin. This was necessary for her protection. In Western Asia today, a woman or girl who is unmarried still becomes prey or a prostitute. Lebanese rape law 522 may have also been an offshoot of the Hammurabi code that forbade men who married women to avoid prosecution from divorcing their victim-wives.

Ancient Egypt was the most progressive place for women. Women were empowered having their own money, homes, land, and resources. There were no formal papers or contracts for marriage or divorce. You lived with someone, had sex, and maybe started a family. Virginity was not necessary for marriage. Men and women could legally divorce. The rules for the union were less complex. This was vastly different from other cultures where not only did a married woman relinquish her right to her own sexuality, if she could not prove a husband's wrongdoing, she would be deported to an isolated island or drowned. Whereas Egyptian women could fight in court, women in other cultures could not. All a man had to do was publicly say he didn't want his wife anymore and that was that. He could divorce her because she couldn't have children or because she burned the toast. Children remained the property of their fathers after divorce.

Today 99% of domestic violence victims remain with their abusers for economic reasons. It wasn't until the 1900's, beginning in and after World War II (1939-1945), that single, divorced, widowed and married American women were able to enter into contracts, own property, collect rents, receive an inheritance, file a lawsuit, be on a jury, and speculate on stock. (Wigington, 2021). Married women in the United States were not able to open bank accounts, apply for credit, or buy or sell property without their husband's signature and consent in many states until the 1960's. The United Nations Report of the Fourth World Conference on Women in September 1995 ascribed the "feminization of poverty" in countries experiencing economic transitions, to rigid social gender roles and "women's limited access to power, education, training, and productive resources." It concluded that due to the "absence of economic opportunities and autonomy, lack of access to economic resources including credit, land ownership, and inheritance, lack of access to education and support services, and their minimal participation in the decision making process, poverty can also force women into situations in which they are vulnerable to sexual exploitation (Cole et al., 2005/2012, pgs. 712-713). During the 2019/2020 coronavirus pandemic, poverty and violence against women and children increased dramatically.

Raised in the Christian tradition, I had been taught that God hated divorce. Marriage was sacrosanct in the church and the vows were supposed to last forever. I learned, however, that this theology comes from the ancient tradition of brides as property. A man could have as many wives and concubines as he wanted or could afford. Polygamy, in most cultures, was not allowed for women. But if you remember, Jesus emancipated women from the bonds put upon them by men. This included freedom from the bondage of abusive marriage.

A contract, a ring, and a ceremony do not a marriage make. When Jesus was asked about divorce, his answer to the teachers of the law was

Moses allowed them to divorce because they were heartless. They were hard, callous, and ruthless. Their offerings and service meant nothing to God because of how they mistreated their wives. In the beginning divorce was not necessary because marriage as we know it, or even as it was known in Jesus' day, did not exist.

If we are to believe the story of Adam and Eve in the first chapter of Genesis, there was no marriage contract or ceremony. There were two people who were naked (vulnerable and open) and unashamed to be who they were, loving each other completely. Marriage originally was an anchor of the soul, twin flames mirroring each other in oneness. There was no need for divorce as one cannot divorce one's self.

If we are to believe history, it will bear out that women were once revered and respected. Greek women, before the advent of both Socrates and Aristotle, were revered for their wisdom and strength. Women walked in the way with Jesus and were integral to the building of the church with Paul. Cleopatra and the Queen of Sheba were not only known for their beauty, but also for their intellect, physical strength, skill in combat, and political savvy. In the beginning, women were honored and respected alongside men. That was and is the design of the creator when he looked at all he created and said, "That's good." We are created equal even though our bodies are different, with the same creativity, authority, and power, including the authority to walk away and divorce ourselves from things that cause us harm.

Male privilege, whether by awareness or ignorance, can put women in bondage to abusive partnerships. Domestic violence and abuse break the original covenant of the oneness of marriage. God loves and is concerned with all parties, including the children, in a marriage. In the timeline of spiritual history, Source never gave manmade institutions first billing.

If Jesus' death is based on the premise that love, not legalities and religious concepts, is paramount to the salvation of humanity, why then would God consign women to the bondage of abusive relationships forever without the grace of divorce?

Men have been controlling the narrative concerning women for thousands of years. The legacy that has been handed down to women from the ancients has been one of subservience, chastity, and domestication. Propaganda in advertising, on social media, in books and magazines would have us believe that women have to be this thin, this tall, this rich to be acceptable. We are told from the bedroom to the boardroom that we are not enough or too much. We look at our bodies in the mirror and hate ourselves because we are too fat, too thin, too dark, too light, too little, too much. We get cosmetic surgeries to build up or tear down. We think twice about stepping into leadership positions, business opportunities, and tech jobs feeling more like an imposter than the CEO, CFO, COO or esteemed scientist. We become less than who we are and who we want to be, living in the shadow of a past we have never seen.

How have women survived and thrived in this hostile environment where law, culture, education, finances, religion, and social order have kept them bound? How do we survive a rape culture where at least 50% of explicit films and adult cartoons viewed by men and boys before the age of 18, depict violent rape of women and young girls? When do we begin having the conversation with our children about abuse and misogyny, what it is, what it looks like, and why it's wrong? When and how do we tell them about the importance of consent and the negative effects of objectification?

Breaking the bonds of abuse involves understanding that there is a history of political, economic, social, academic, and religious sanctioning regarding disenfranchisement of women and girls that must be addressed. All of us, at one point or another, have been affected. Women have been living with the ancients so long and been eaten alive without realizing that the infestation that has continued to grow and evolve, was built into the structure of our lives, our beliefs about who we are as women and girls, and what our place is in society. Systemic, structural gender inequality has been part of our inheritance from ancient civilizations, but all is not lost.

There is an old adage that states, "If you don't know your history, you are doomed to repeat it." With knowledge comes the power to effect change. If we are to overcome our circumstances, we must recognize what we are up against historically so that we can effectively arm ourselves for the fight of and for our lives. With knowledge, we can use wisdom to act upon what we know. Some ways we can act are:

- Visit women's organizations in your community. Find out what the issues for women are where you live and how they are being addressed. Volunteer for a cause or effort you belive in.
- Come to the aide of your sisters in other countries by supporting fair trade or donating to girls education.
- Take a self-defense or boxing class. Teach your daughters how to fight like Spartans and rule their own lives like queens. Teach them how to protect themselves physically and how to fight in boardrooms, classrooms, education, science, technology, and government. Enlist credible mentors.
- Go online and sign up for state and federal meetings that discuss women's issues. The Sunshine Act gives the public the legal right to attend. Get knowledge and support those in government who stand against domestic violence, sex trafficking, and assault.

- Speak up. Talk to local government officials and find out what they are doing about laws in your state and community concerning rape and domestic violence. Ask your state and federal representatives what is happening with the Violence Against Women Act that continues to sit on the senate floor. Send letters, draft petitions.

- Speak up for yourself when going to see physicians and seeking treatment. Don't be afraid to ask your doctor questions and demand answers when it comes to your mental and physical health. If you are not satisfied with the answer or the doctor, move on to someone who genuinely has your interest at heart. Too many times we say nothing, and thousands of unnecessary surgeries, illegal sterilizations, and hysterectomies have been done on women because we have been taught to accept the word of an authority in silence. Silence is not always golden.

- Learn the rules of your state concerning divorce, marital rape, legal separation, abortion, planned parenthood, whatever rules apply to women and girls in your community, state, and federal government. The more informed you are, the better choices you will be able to make concerning yourself and your family, especially before and after marriage.

- Call your local domestic abuse hotline (see phone numbers in the resources in the back of the book) if you are in an abusive situation or just want to understand someone who is. If you are being abused, talk to people you trust and those you can rely on to help you and keep your information private. Get help developing a safety plan for yourself and those you love.

- Act. Help women in a shelter by volunteering your time. If you suspect someone is dealing with domestic violence, let them know you are there for them. Don't try to force them to talk or share. They have to trust you for that. Just give them information if you can and let them know you are there for them if they need someone to listen. Be a safe place for a child dealing with abuse at home. Leave information about domestic violence in church bathrooms and public facilities. Learn, teach, and share as much as you can that will benefit others. Don't judge. You may not be in a situation or have ever experienced abuse. This never gives you the right to judge others who have.

- Have the conversation with your sons and daughters about how human beings should treat one another in relationships, no matter how difficult the conversation may be. Educate yourself and your children about abuse, what it looks like, how to keep themselves as safe as possible. Learn about teen dating violence (see resources in the back of the book) and how to teach children about safety. Connect with any domestic abuse projects in your area to get additional information and assistance.

- Sex trafficking and domestic violence increases in times of disaster, economic hardship, sudden shifts in family or partner dynamics including the loss or birth of a child. If you see something, say something.

- Be a part of the solution. Become a change maker. You can change history for yourself and your generations.

It's Alright to be Angry

Be angry and sin not. — Ephesians 4:26a (KJV)

A sin is anything that you do which goes against yourself. Everything you feel or believe or say that goes against yourself is a sin. — Don Miguel Ruiz,

I used to wonder what the scriptures meant when I read, "Be angry and sin not." I wondered how in the world you can be angry and not sin. As a church kid I was taught that being angry was a sin. I learned that sin is anything we do against God. What was coded as sin, however, was based on what particular church you belonged to. When I was younger, for example, being brought up in the Pentecostal tradition, it was a sin for women to wear pants. I never quite understood this, questioned it often, and was called rebellious for doing so. Was questioning also a sin? Did questioning mean I was rebellious? Would I go to hell for wanting an answer, for wanting to know? Was my brain sinful?

Wearing red dresses was also a sin. Red is my favorite color. To my mother's mortification, at 16, I bought a red wrap, cap sleeved, just above the knee length dress, showed up late to church, and pranced all around the sanctuary in my four-inch heels. Mom couldn't get out of the choir box to address me. I laughed smugly to myself when an usher told me my mom wanted me to sit down. Years later, women wearing pants in the church where I grew up, was no longer a sin. Neither was wearing red, wearing dresses above the ankle or even above the knee, dating without the intention of getting married, wearing anything sleeveless, wearing jeans, going to the movies, dancing, and a plethora of other don'ts that had become okay. What changed? Did God no longer care about those things?

The word sin, as we know it, is derived from the Old English meaning guilty. When I was younger, I was guilty of wearing pants. I was guilty of rebelling against what I did not believe in, what could not be proven, and what didn't make sense. I debated with my Sunday school teachers-one a pastor, the other a deacon- about women wearing pants. They postulated that the Bible says women should not wear men's garments. I answered that neither men nor women wore pants in those days so how did women wearing pants become a thing? The subject came around to the taboo of dancing. All dancing outside of "getting the spirit" was forbidden. An astute Bible scholar, I countered with; David danced before the Lord with all his might. We don't know if David was doing the cabbage patch, the two step, hava nagilah, or just making it up as he went. We know he danced himself out of his clothes. After class, they told my mom that I needed to be in an adult class. That was a subtle way of kicking me out so I wouldn't influence any other young people to ask questions. I was 15.

I bought my first pair of pants, a pair of jeans made by *Itsy-Bitsy* in a size double zero, at age eighteen. I still had an 18-inch waist and weighed less than 100 pounds. I was so proud of those pants. Mom said I could not wear them in her house. I respected her rules. I would go around the corner to my auntie's, put my pants on, and go on about my business. When it was time to go home, I would go to my aunt's or my cousin's, change back into my skirt, and go home.

Me? Rebellious? It was true. What did wearing makeup, earrings, lipstick, dancing, and red dresses have to do with God loving and caring for me? It seemed like God had a whole list of things that you would have to pay for in hell jail if you did them. In my mind, God was extremely judgmental and no fun at all.

That rebellious part of me never changed. According to the religious doctrine I grew up with, God hated homosexuality, sex before marriage, shacking or living with a partner before marriage, same sex marriage, and divorce. In fact, according to religious doctrine, God hated divorce so much that he demanded women stay in abusive relationships and live in such a way that they transform their husbands, making victims responsible for their spouse's behavior. Yes, I rebelled and fought against that too.

It was exceedingly difficult for me to choose to not only leave my abusive husband, but to also leave the church I was attending at the time and divorce them both. I had been raised in church and had become a member of only two churches my entire life. Once upon a time, I believed and accepted what I had been told about divorce and God's judgement. This was my second marriage. After my first divorce, I had been told by church folks that no one was going to want me. As a divorced Christian woman, I was damaged goods. No one was going to marry a divorced woman because that was a sin against God.

I was walking around with all this guilt and condemnation. Then I got married again. As the marriage became increasingly unhealthy, I wrestled with the spiritual implications of leaving my husband. I prayed and sought pastoral counseling. No matter how much more abusive my husband became, I was strongly encouraged to stay and pray. One Sunday the pastor called him out before the church. I thought he would be openly reprimanded, that this would finally be his day of reckoning. Instead, he was praised before the congregation for his evangelical work and the pastor announced that she was going to ordain him as a minister. The pastor looked directly at me as she made the announcement. Instead of correcting him, she sanctioned his behavior by elevating him. I felt utterly dismissed and silenced.

My teenagers did not want to go to church anymore. They had reported the abuse in our home to youth leaders. They too were hushed, silenced, and ignored. I left the church where I had been a committed member for over 15 years and, for a brief time, attended another church outside of our community where my children and I could exist as strangers. Not comfortable with the teaching or the environment there, I resorted to television ministries and a stream of peaceful instrumental worship music to help me sleep at night. Sometimes I sent my younger children to church with their father. Most times they stayed home with me.

My favorite television minister was Dr. Joyce Meyer. She had been abused so I felt she would understand someone like me. I wrote to her and two other ministers I watched on television. Two of those ministries didn't bother answering my letter, but instead sent me requests for donations, sales brochures to buy their materials and books, and envelopes to send in money or join a prayer chain at cost. I was horrified and disappointed. I felt that these two ministers, one teaching on prosperity and the other famous for his beautiful glass cathedral, cared nothing about my plight.

Joyce Meyer, however, wrote me a personal heartwarming letter, sent me some materials on domestic violence and abuse, some of her speaking tapes on the subject, and several books, all at no cost. She did this not once, but twice even though my only other correspondence with her was a thank you note. Her sincere concern, attention and information helped me to understand domestic violence more from a spiritual perspective. The information she shared was instrumental in helping me to break free of the code of silence surrounding domestic violence, abuse, and toxic religion. My husband worked night shift every two weeks, so I took that time to learn more and pray with my feet moving, developing a safety plan, saving money, and earning money in a network marketing business, all in secret.

I told my pastor, in writing, that I was formally resigning from church membership, and I was leaving my husband. She contacted my husband immediately and demanded he come to meet with her concerning me. Thankfully, she didn't go into detail and my husband refused to meet with her contending that he was not going to go listen to something stupid I had obviously done. Twenty-four hours later, my children and I were gone.

There were other people who poured into my life during this time. After reading the book, *All the Joy You Can Stand* by Debrena Jackson Gandy, I wrote to the author. She was speaking at a conference in Atlanta, Georgia. That conference had a session on domestic violence given by the nation's leading authority on the subject. I wrote to Ms. Gandy telling her how much I enjoyed her book, how it spoke to me and that, though I wouldn't be able to attend the event, I had been moved and empowered by what she had written. I also shared a little of my story. She sent me tickets to the event, paid in full, and $500 for the cost of the flight and hotel. I wept uncontrollably.

I was bound by the scripture, "What God hath joined together, let no man put asunder." A friend of my mother who happened to be a Christian counselor gave me words of wisdom that freed me. She said, "We often mistake what God hath joined for what we have joined, and God is not obligated to keep your marriage if he didn't join you." That was news to me. I understood then that a dress, a ring, a piece of paper, some words and a ceremony do not make a marriage. I remembered signs from Spirit telling me not to marry my husband. I remembered having prophetic dreams about the marriage during the engagement. I did not heed the warnings. God had not joined us. We had made a bargain with one another, two lonely, scared, scarred, fractured individuals who had not fully healed from their past united in a matrimony that was anything but holy.

Leaving my abusive marriage was not easy. As a Christian woman, I had to contend with beliefs about sinning against and losing the favor of God. I felt I had to choose between God and protecting myself and my family. My husband had threatened to kill me, and I believed he could with what, to him, was justification. I had to learn to live with being labeled rebellious, that word I had heard used against me so many times in my youth by my mother, pastors, and other church folk when I didn't go along to get along. I was tired of being everyone's scapegoat.

I have since learned that religious doctrine is capricious, changing according to who holds power and influence and what those people want to achieve. I am rebellious. I answer to it now because I understand and accept rebellion as an act of open resistance against someone or something that is attempting to establish control over me. I chose to no longer be under the control of someone who disrespected me, intentionally hurt and demeaned me, played psychological head games, economically disenfranchised me, and generally terrorized the household. This is not the will or plan of God for anyone's life. I chose to rebel against such terror.

We close our eyes to things we do not want to acknowledge when we want something. We pretend that the piece of chocolate cake, potato chips and ice cream will not add pounds to our waistline or affect our health. We say we'll work out an extra half hour at the gym and we know we won't go. We make new year's resolutions that we seldom, if ever, keep. We lie to ourselves and on ourselves about the agreements or contracts we make with ourselves and others. We will not be free from those contracts unless we tell the truth.

Processing truth can be agonizing. The truth was even though the pastor had joined my husband and I in a ceremony, even though the state had granted us a license, no matter how many witnesses were present, our marriage had not been God's brainchild. It had been ours. The truth was that I had become "faithful Kim" not only because I was always one to give 110%, but because I had also become a people pleaser needing approval and acceptance. I had ceased worshipping God, and had begun instead, to worship a human being. I had to address doctrines I had become complicit in propagating that were not factual and/or truly spiritually based. I had to acknowledge that the religion, specifically the church I was involved in, had become toxic. Coming to grips with all of this had me prostrate on the hardwood floor in my bedroom, my hands fisted so tight my nails dug into my palms, a deluge of tears scattered over the floor, my stomach quaking and lurching, nausea ripping at my throat. I had to vomit all the deceptions I had accepted as God's honest truth. I had to come to grips with myself and my complicity in my situation. I took the pain of giving birth to a new self, the anguish worse than any discomfort I ever felt giving birth to my five children.

We wrestle with this question of sin. The original meaning is derived from the Latin denoting error, transgression, or lapse in judgement. Don Miguel Ruiz may have considered this when he said, "Sin begins with the rejection of yourself. Self-rejection is the biggest sin that you commit" (Ruiz & Mills, 1997, pg. 31). This had nothing to do with guilt.

Ultimately, it is the agreements, the contracts we make with ourselves and others that shape our lives. The sin we most often commit is against ourselves. It is the sin of making agreements with ourselves and others that are not in our best interest. It is not saying what we really want, how we really feel, what we really believe. It is accepting what does not benefit us spiritually, physically, financially, psychologically, emotionally, and economically. I made agreements with myself to enter into relationships in my personal life that made me feel less than. When I dug deep, I realized that I had signed spiritual contracts to discount myself based on words that had been said to me early on. Because I believed, accepted, and got into agreement with the negative words that were spoken to me and over me, I unconsciously sought out unhealthy, unproductive relationships that were not what I really wanted. These relationships were based on negative programming I had gotten in agreement with.

Every time someone calls you stupid, ugly, mean, a bitch, a whore, and you accept those words, you make an internal agreement with yourself that works against you. Every time someone blames you for their behavior and you accept the blame by second-guessing yourself, you make an internal agreement with yourself that works against you. Every time you accept what you do not want, you make an agreement with yourself that works against you. The universe will then continue to give you those things that work against you according to all the agreements you have made with yourself. When you renew your mind, you can then change your agreements which will in turn change your life.

God is not going to make decisions for you. He is not angry with you for choosing. He gave you a brain, a will, and power. He is not intervening with any of that. The will of man is as powerful as the will of God in the earth. Will is derived from the future tense; what we, humankind, wills to happen. Power is the ability to make things happen. If you have willpower, you have been endowed with the power to make things happen. Source endowed us, from the beginning of time, to make things happen in the future. He would never take that away. He does not condemn any of our choices. There is no decision you make that he will not lead and guide you through if you will allow it. Stay or go. Suffer or survive. Survive or thrive. It's all the same to him and he will not condemn you. The truth is it is going to be hard no matter what you choose. But he promised to be with you. He didn't promise you would feel his presence. He didn't promise he would make your load any lighter or easier. He promised he would be there, right beside you. When you suffer, he will suffer. When you cry, he will be there catching your tears.

When I chose to leave my husband, Hebrews 13:5b kept repeating in my spirit; "for He has said, "I will never [under any circumstances] desert you [nor give you up nor leave you without support, nor will I in any degree leave you helpless], nor will I forsake or let you down or relax my hold on you [assuredly not] (Amplified Bible)!

We have the perception that God is angry with us and we, in turn, are angry with God. There are no prerequisites for the love and presence of Spirit. It just is. You and your choices are accepted without condemnation. We cannot choose for anyone else, nor can we change their choices by our "chaste behavior." If threats and fear tactics are working for an abuser, doing the best you can to please him or her will not make a difference.

God is not angry with us. He does not take his love from us, nor does he bring wrath upon us for making choices like divorce and ending partnerships to save our lives and the lives of our offspring. He is also not mad at us if we choose to stay. Either way, God will be with you. The situation you are in may not change, but if you are impeccable with your word to yourself, you will change in the situation. Not for the sake of your husband or your children, but for you own integrity.

The day I looked in the mirror and did not recognize me, I made the choice to change. My situation was the same. I did not leave my husband immediately. My husband did not change, and I no longer required him to. I worked on me. I had always believed in purpose and destiny, and I knew the life I was living was not true to what I believed. I was not being impeccable with my word to myself. It was up to me to change that.

To be impeccable means to be without sin. To be without sin means to live, speak, and act with words and deeds that are true to you. Do yourself no harm. Be faultless with your words about yourself. Speak to yourself with kindness and compassion. Be honest with yourself. No matter who is saying what against you, be honest with yourself. Be rebellious and do yourself no harm.

I understand now that you can be angry and without sin. Anger is necessary if you want to get your power and your energy back. You will have to come to a place of white hot anger, not with others, but with yourself and what you have accepted for your life. That is difficult, to say the least. Stop accepting anything, not words, not choices, not doctrine, which go against yourself. It is well with your soul for you to be angry about the contracts and agreements you have accepted that go against yourself, even if they are sanctioned by social constructs and religious beliefs. Anger is not then a sin, but a salvation. Until you get angry, you will continue to tolerate things you hate. Until you get angry, you will continue to accept being demeaned. Until you get angry with yourself and your situation, you will continue to make the same choices on repeat, attracting the same kind of people, the same kind of energy to your life. Anger is necessary to move you forward. To keep you from sinning against yourself.

I never said recovering yourself would be easy.

Gaslighting 101

Lies don't end relationships. The truth does. — Shannon L. Alder

Dr. Elaine Weiss, Ed.D., said , "Abuse is not a slap, a punch, or a curse. Abuse is a campaign. A vigorous concerted effort to accomplish a purpose. A process of deliberate intimidation intended to coerce the victim to do the will of the victimizer"(Weiss, 2000). Like a political campaign, gaslighting has three things in common:

1. The creation and promotion of specific messages. In a political campaign, the candidate shares a message with the voters, something he wants his constituents to believe and get on board with. This message is repeated frequently in order to leave an indelible impression on the minds of those who hear it, whether the message is true or not. The abuser has a message he wants to leave ingrained in the victim's mind. It is often a message of inadequacy, lack of intelligence, poor memory, ineptness, clumsiness, poor body image, sexual inability, prudishness, unattractiveness, unloveliness, or any other twisted communication the victimizer can get his victim and those associated with the victim, to accept as truth.

2. The candidate courts special interest groups to get on board with his or her campaign messages. In an abusive relationship these groups can be your family, his family, your boss, employees, co-workers, his boss, his employees, his co-workers, your pastor, rabbi, priest, friends, and people you both know and admire. He needs this audience to co-sign his campaign, so he repeatedly and charismatically shares the same negative message in his most charming voice with them.

3. The candidate has a well thought out plan, an organized strategy of propaganda, recruitment, and public relations. The gaslighter knows exactly what his goal is; to gain and maintain control. Nothing he does is accidental. He skews the message to get you off balance, so you begin questioning yourself, becoming dependent on him for the supposed "truth." He recruits others who believe his message and question your perception, ideas,

thoughts, and reasoning causing you to question yourself about what is true or false. The gaslighter sets in motion a highly organized public relations campaign to isolate you from others whose professional opinions, insights, knowledge, and wisdom you may trust and those who may genuinely love you and want to help you.

Gaslighting is mind control, a mental sleight of hand. Like a magician's trick, the abuser attempts to distort, minimize, and control what the victim says, sees, hears, and feels. It is psychological sabotage and emotional manipulation. Gaslighting is a game of dirty pool where you are constantly the mark.

The term gaslighting originates from a stage play, *Gas Light*, produced in 1938, filmed in 1940 and 1944. In the story a husband attempts to drive his wife crazy by an insidious campaign of denial and lies causing his wife to believe she is hopelessly mentally ill. He courts special interest groups like their friends, her family, their staff to get on board with his "diagnosis" by constantly telling them his wife is "sick." He has a well-planned strategy, pretending he did not say or do any of the things that she plainly sees, hears, knows, and understands until she begins believing what he says is true. He isolates her so that no one can see his dirty work, figure out his scheme, or tell her what is really happening.

Gaslighting is psychological warfare bent on breaking the victim's will by distorting her reality, self-perception, self-reliance, self-worth, self-love, and self-esteem, sending the victim off balance for a moment or for a lifetime. An abuser uses gaslighting as a means of keeping his victim emotionally and psychologically dependent. Victims question their own feelings, instincts, reality, and their sanity giving the victimizer incredible power over them.

One evening my husband, we'll call him Peter, called from work and asked that I make fish and rice for dinner. I did as he requested. When he came home, dinner was hot and ready on the stove. I was satisfied this would make him happy. He came into the kitchen, looked at the meal and said, "I asked you to make chicken." I said, "No you didn't." We went back and forth with this for a minute before he exploded saying, "Yes I did. I don't know what's wrong with your brain. I told you I wanted chicken! I'm not eating that." He stormed out of the kitchen and up the stairs. I stood there looking at the meal I had prepared. Did he ask for chicken instead of fish? Did I hear him wrong? I could swear he said fish. I wrote it down. But maybe he did say chicken and I was thinking fish. What was wrong with me? I blamed myself rather than think for a moment Peter could intentionally be messing with my head. This type of thing went on so often it threw me off balance as was intended, causing me to constantly second guess myself and my intentions for several years.

On another occasion, Peter and I were lying in bed. I was lying on my left side in the fetal position, as I often did, falling asleep. Peter lay behind me. He pressed his thumb deep and hard into a bruise I had on my right thigh. When I cried out in pain, he said, "What's wrong with you?" I told him what he did. He said he didn't do it. After a few minutes, he pressed his thumb deep into the wound again. When I told him to stop, he said, "Stop what?" A few minutes later, he proceeded to do the same thing a third time. Moving over and out of his reach, I yelled at him. He shouted at me for accusing him of starting an argument over something he never did!

A few months after the birth of our last child, Peter asked me what I would do if he ever hit me. I told him that I would not try to fight him as he is taller and stronger than me. I also promised him, however, that he would never be able to go to sleep in our home again. I did not flinch when I said it because I meant it.

Peter's behavior towards me up to that point had been strictly verbal and aimed only at me – accusations and derogatory remarks, criticism of my family and friends, temper tantrums that included throwing things at me, and threats of physical violence. I was physically fit and extremely strong for my tiny build. I had also grown up wrestling with my older brothers, so I was not moved by the threat of violence. There was something about someone putting their hands on me to harm me that triggered me in extreme ways. I was ruthless in a physical fight and wasn't afraid to go mano-a-mano if I had to. I knew that about myself. Peter figured that out about me.

When you are dating, you tell your partner a lot about you. As intimacy increases, you tell your partner your secrets, your biggest fears, your biggest failures. You share your weaknesses, your strengths, your heart. An abuser who is narcissistic or sociopathic listens well, storing all this information away to use against you when convenient. My husband knew of my recurring nightmares of being raped. He knew I had been molested in my childhood. He knew I had been sexually assaulted and stalked as an adult. He knew rape was my biggest fear and frequent nightmare. When threats of hitting me did not get the results he aimed for, he used what he knew would have a greater impact.

The first time it happened I was in shock. I still have trouble calling it rape. I told Peter he was hurting me. I screamed, cried, and pleaded with him to stop. When I told him how I felt afterwards, he called me frigid and said he thought I was screaming and crying because I liked it.

Sex with Peter wasn't always like that. I loved making love with him. The cuddling, stroking his head while he lay on my chest, massaging his back, lying on his chest listening to his heartbeat while he held me close, were part and parcel of all those little things that come with making love. We were good together, which is why the unexpected bouts of sexual violence and debasement always threw me. Things would start out normal and escalate or start with anger and end with him stroking my hair, calling me beautiful.

There were many episodes of demeaning sexual behavior thereafter to the point I could not walk without acute vaginal pain. My gynecologist who I had been seeing for several years was shocked and angry when he examined me, interrogating me, taking me to his office to privately speak with me after the examination. He was a kind and caring doctor; someone I had met years before while working at a hospital, someone I trusted. When he questioned me, I was afraid and ashamed, so I lied about what was happening to me. He offered to help me. I assured him there was no need, there was nothing wrong. I was afraid that Peter might be arrested and go to jail or be questioned and not taken in custody. Either way, I might be at further risk. Concerned, the doctor prescribed medication for the pain and let me go, his hands tied by patient-doctor privilege and HIPPA law. He had delivered two of my five babies. I never went to see him again.

I was in denial and confused for a long time, blaming myself, thinking there was something wrong with me. I could not conceive of someone loving me and intentionally hurting me at the same time. What I thought about what was happening didn't make sense. I felt like I was losing my mind. Peter had found the key to bending my will, keeping me afraid, insecure, and off balance. Once he knew how to keep me subjected to him, the abuse and gaslighting escalated. He called me stupid once. My response was so cutting and lethal he never called me stupid directly again but would insinuate with statements like; "What were you thinking? Where are your brains? You must be out of your mind." When I would react to his insults he would say, "You can't take a joke. You're always overreacting. You're too sensitive. Why are you always so dramatic?" I was dazed by the stories he concocted, stunned by the quick jabs and snide remarks, confused by the outright lies, subtle deceptions and innuendos, the games he played to gain power over me and knock me off balance.

It wasn't always words. Sometimes it was a look. Something as simple as a raised eyebrow or a glint in his eye could mean more than anyone else could readily assess. That look was just for me.

I had been raised on an elusive perfection so I kept trying to get it right, that thing that would satisfy him, make him as loving, attentive, and kind as he had been when we were first dating. I was also in deep denial. It could not be true that the man I fell in love with could be purposefully cruel and deceitful.

It was our fifth anniversary. I asked Peter what he thought was the purpose of marriage. He said, "A woman is supposed to submit to her husband, and when she doesn't, he is to discipline her." At that point, I knew nothing would change. He had spoken what he deeply believed. I was exhausted, overwhelmed, depressed, and contemplating taking my life. I became self-destructive, doing things that I knew would make Peter angry or upset. I wanted him to hit me and get it over with. I wanted the fight. I was tired of the threats. When I told my pastor what was happening, I ended up questioning myself more. I was not being submissive, that's why he did the things he did. I was too rebellious. If I would just do right, be right, get right things would change. None of that was right. Peter's behavior was not my fault, but I didn't know or understand that at the time.

Abuse never happens in a vacuum. Your abuser is not just gaslighting you. He is doing the same, with charm and finesse, to others. His deceit is so well disguised, people see you as the problem. You are ungrateful, incompetent, whorish, devilish, a liar, a thief, suspect. He has successfully made you the villain in the drama he created to protect himself from his own insecurities. He tells you that no one will believe you and you can never get away from him. He fabricates and exaggerates character weaknesses, telling you everyone knows you're a drama queen, sick in the head, stupid, dull, dumb, flirty, mean, self-absorbed. Your gaslighter has told you what and how you think. My husband used to say, "You don't know what you think" and "You don't think that." You withdraw from family, friends, and community embarrassed and ashamed because you believe the lies that have been imbedded deep in your psyche, in your spirit, until your actions are controlled by untrue beliefs. You do not go to people for help because you are afraid of being judged and criticized for not being stronger, a better person, perfect, or that he will find out and harm you or your children. You isolate yourself because you are ashamed, depressed, anxious. You feel alone.

The one thing that helped me to wake up and become aware that I was in an abusive relationship was access to information. I didn't know or understand what was happening to me. I had never heard of gaslighting. I knew my heart ached for the man that had swept me off my feet before the wedding bells rang. I believed he was in there somewhere and I tried everything in my power to get him out and into the open again. He would show up during the honeymoon phase, but I learned later that was only a ruse to lull me into a false sense of security.

They say knowledge is power. Once I educated myself on the subject of abuse, deep diving into research on domestic violence in all its forms, I was empowered. There was such a paradigm shift, my husband felt it. I could give a name to what was happening to me. I finally had the playbook. I was acutely aware of the campaign.

Escalation usually occurs either when the victim has decided to leave, to fight back, or when the abuser feels he is losing control. I was coming out of my bedroom when Peter intentionally shoved me causing me to fall against the side of the wall. There was plenty of room for both of us to easily fit through the door together. "Why'd you push me?" I asked. Smiling, he denied shoving me and asked what I was talking about. I knew his intentional thrust meant a further escalation of his abusive behavior. I knew it was a test and there would be more like it with increasing intensity. I could have argued with Peter. Instead, I said nothing and continued going about my business. Gaslighting, sexual assault, psychological battery, economic abuse had all been a part of my life with Peter up to that point. I knew the physical battery he was introducing with a shove would not bode well for any of us.

Lord Acton said in 1887, "Power tends to corrupt and absolute power corrupts absolutely." When you are in a gaslighting relationship, you give up your power and allow someone else to lead your life. One of my favorite poets, Alice Walker, said "The most common way people give up their power is by thinking they don't have any." When you are in a gaslighting relationship, whether it be with parents, siblings, other relatives, so called friends, a partner, a spouse, a social group, or religious organization, you believe the lie that you are powerless. When you find out the truth, it changes you. It changes your perspective. It changes your inward motivation. It changes your perception. It shifts you from where you are to where you want to be.

Once I learned the truth, once I got the information I needed, I began to plan. After my husband shoved me, I knew the most loving thing I could do for myself, my husband, and my children was to take us all out of a potentially explosive situation.

When you are in an abusive gaslighting relationship, you become someone you were never meant to be. I became as enraged and volatile as my husband, staging small acts of rebellion. He demanded I scratch his back one early evening. This was not unusual as he had dry skin and, early on, I had often scratched his back for him. This, however, had become a tedious chore, the demands lasting for hours until he fell asleep. When I would go to sleep, he would wake me up to start again. It would also occur at times I was busy with the children, or trying to fix dinner, write, read, or get anything meaningful done. I was his wife and as such was in service whenever he demanded. This time, sitting on the edge of the bed where he lay, I looked at my long, sharp, painted nails and, like a tiger in the cartoons whose claws come out with a loud "zing," I dug deep into his flesh and pulled from his shoulders to the base of his spine in a swift stinging motion. His back involuntary arched. He gasped and stared at me, his face contorted between fury, surprise, and pain. Skin and blood were in my nails. I sat there glaring back at him. He looked away, calling me crazy. Silently, I got up, went down to the kitchen, washed my hands, and returned to tending to the children.

I had never owned a car or had one inspected. My husband took care of both the old Dodge Caravan I drove that smoked like a chimney, and the sexy Park Avenue he had insisted upon getting with our income tax refund, which he drove. When I asked how the van passed inspection, he accused me of listening to some other man. He got in my face and yelled asking me who I had been talking to, who was I fooling around with behind his back. Two days before my children and I left, I was pulled over by the police for an illegal inspection sticker. The police officer scraped the sticker off the vehicle and told me to drive home. Home was at least

25 to 30 miles away. He confirmed there was a strong possibility I would get pulled over by other police officers and get more tickets or have the vehicle confiscated on the way. I had no doubt Peter had gotten the van inspected illegally on purpose.

I drove to my parents' home and told them what happened. My stepfather, after my mother calmed him down, followed me home to make sure the children and I were safe should I get stopped. When we got home, my husband was upstairs asleep. I fed the children, put them to bed, and confronted him. When I told him about the fake inspection sticker, he first directed his anger toward the technician he had hired. By morning, he blamed me, calling me irresponsible and unappreciative. He threatened to take the van and warned me that the children and I would go back to walking and taking the bus everywhere. I took his hand, opened it, put the keys to the van in his palm closing his hand over them and calmly walked away. Neither the van nor the car was in my name though it was primarily my money that had purchased both. I knew the van could be traced by way of a license plate and leaving it was already part of my safety plan. My days of fighting him were over.

These small acts of rebellion had Peter coming home from work in the middle of the day. He worked on an assembly line. Employees were not allowed to leave until their shift was over, not even for lunch. Peter was trying to clock my every move. He had witnessed the shift in my attitude and actions. I had stopped fighting him. I think he sensed that I was going to leave him.

A psychological abuser is the master of manipulation. They are great storytellers, always spinning the narrative to their point of view. Your partner revels in starting senseless arguments in order to get you upset and take you off course. He tells you that your friends and family are judging you, so you don't seek help, so you distrust them and rely solely on him. He tells you his physical abuse is all in your mind, something you made up, and there is something wrong with your mind, you are crazy. He pretends not to understand what you are saying. He insults and humiliates you then says you can't take a joke when you react, calling you oversensitive, dramatic, and stupid.

A person who gaslights you has ulterior motives for attempting to define your reality. Sometimes he does it for pure entertainment. Other times he does it because he feels inferior or threatened. Someone who gaslights you needs control of your emotions in order to control your perception. Gaslighting is about invalidating your experiences thus forcing you to see things the way the abuser intends. It screws with the reality of what happened to you, who you are, and what you think. A gaslighter needs control of your relationships with others so there is no outside influence. He needs control of your habits so he can lead you into new habits you may never be able to break. He may introduce alcohol, drugs, orgies, even prostitution to take you off course or create an addiction. If he finds and knows your buttons, he will push every single one.

Gaslighting is about mind control. The goal is to render victims so dispirited and dysfunctional they are malleable and unable to fight back. Studies have shown that psychological abuse can be more damaging and long lasting than any other abusive behavior. Gas-lighting is about controlling an individual's thoughts and thus their behaviors. Constant exposure to gas-lighting can lead to mental illness, post-traumatic stress, anxiety, depression, suicidal ideation, and suicide completion. When you have been gaslighted, decision making becomes incredibly cloudy. Your thoughts don't seem to come together like they used to. You feel scattered, lost, helpless, powerless.

Gaslighting is a tactic commonly used in the campaigns of abusers, narcissists, sociopaths, cult leaders, authoritarians, and dictators. It is a hostile takeover rendering its victims dysfunctional and struggling to recover. But recovery is possible. All is not lost. The first step is awareness and education.

I knew something was happening to me. I couldn't explain it, couldn't put my finger on it until I read a brochure on domestic violence. Like a diagnosis in a doctor's office, I could finally give a name to the thing that was making me lose my mind. Once I knew the diagnosis, I learned how to treat it.

I started my recovery campaign by changing the messaging I was giving to myself. I used affirmations I wrote down on file cards, reading them three to four times a day to renew my mind. I reprogrammed myself to think more positively about myself, to disseminate the untrue beliefs I had been living my life by. To change my self-perception. This is strong medicine. Your subconscious works by exposure and repetition. I had been conditioned to hate myself and not know myself. There were limiting beliefs from my childhood and adulthood that I had received in my psyche as truth. My subconscious was acting on autopilot. I had to change that. I had to break agreements in my subconscious mind that said I was stupid, ugly, unlovable, a devil, sneaky, a thief, dirty, mean, a failure. Thoughts that would shout at me whenever I made a mistake, suffered a loss, or faced a challenge. I destroyed those words and beliefs by changing my thought life. I stopped getting in agreement with words spoken against me, words I spoke against myself. I began agreeing with words that affirmed me in every area of my life. This empowered and strengthened me to take other action required to move forward. These tools helped me to recover myself.

The realization of what was happening to me was paramount to my recovery. One of the things that helped was keeping a journal. By recording my daily activities, including my thoughts and anything that happened to me that day, I could validate what I saw, heard, and felt giving credence to my reality. By recording things as they happened, and keeping my journals in a safe place, I not only captured my memories with time and date; I also had evidence should I need it in court. You can also take pictures, date stamp them, and keep them in a safe place. I would urge against keeping them on your phone or any place your abuser has access. You can print them from a phone and store them elsewhere.

I took advantage of hotlines for women against rape, domestic violence, and suicide prevention. (See resources at the end of this book.) It helped to talk it out anonymously with someone who was in no way connected to me. Growing up we were told that anything that happened in the house stayed in the house. You didn't air your "dirty laundry." You kept your grievances to yourself. The hotlines' policies of anonymity created a safe distance between myself and the person who answered the call which, in turn, made me feel secure that I wasn't endangering my life or someone else's by "tattle-telling." It also helped to validate my feelings and memory.

If possible, I also recommend enlisting the help of a psychologist or psychiatrist. Both are good listeners that can help you navigate your mental health. A psychiatrist can dispense medication if needed. Thanks to my therapists, I was able to recognize my own co-dependent behavioral habits and isolating patterns. I learned my spouse's particular gaslighting habits and, eventually, became immune to most of them. This allowed me to re-establish broken relationships, come out of isolation, establish new boundaries for myself, and move forward. Make sure you are comfortable with your therapist. Some therapists have control issues too. If you feel you are not being heard or are in any way uncomfortable, try someone else. You are not obligated to stay under any one person's care because they have doctor in front of their name.

You cannot change a person that abuses, neglects, or mistreats you. Recovery is not about the other person. Recovery is for you. The effects of gaslighting are far reaching and often long term. Like an alcoholic or a drug addict, you will always need to go back and use your tools. Depending on how long you have been exposed to gaslighting, the penetration of negative thoughts and untrue beliefs may go very deep but by recognizing the signs and symptoms of gaslighting and treating them accordingly, you can recover.

God Bless the Child

We worry about what a child will become tomorrow, yet we forget that he is someone today. — Stacia Tauscher

Momma may have. Poppa may have. But God bless the child that's got his own. That's got his own. — Billie Holiday.

Every good parent wants what is best for their children even when they don't know what that is. We want our children to grow up to be healthy, whole, happy, compassionate, independent human beings. Our children, in turn, want to be loved, praised, adored, nurtured, and accepted. No matter how screwed up we parents are, our children want to please us. They want to be just like mommy or daddy or somewhere in between them both. They stake their lives on what we say and do.

Ryan, my youngest and not his real name, was closest to his father, constantly watching him, desiring only to follow in his footsteps. From the time he was about two years old, Peter would take Ryan with him to clients' homes when he cut hair. He would give Ryan a dollar for sweeping up afterwards. Ryan adored his father and the special times they often spent working, eating a forbidden treat before dinner, and laughing together. When he was three, he asked his then four-year-old sister Tina, not her real name, to help him get dressed. He wanted to wear a suit jacket and shoes like his dad. Tina dressed him in an undershirt, a button down shirt, and two vests – a knitted one and a fabric one. He wore his little tan suit jacket and his big brother's socks stuffed into his own loafers. Tina introduced him, proudly showing off her four year old fashion skills. He strutted before me holding the lapels of his suit jacket, head high, a huge smile spread across his bright young face, his light brown eyes shining with joy. It was at least 80 degrees in the house. He was sweating like a pig on a roaster, but he fought me tooth and nail when I tried undressing him. He wanted to look like his dad. He was adamant about that.

My little girls were no different. They loved to put on mommy's makeup, perfume, jewelry, clothes, and walk around in my high heels, tripping and staggering as they went, happy blurred lipstick smiles on their faces.

Like their parents, my children wanted to be and do lots of things. Among them there were dreams of being a carpenter, an artist, an architect, a fashion designer, a poet, a "rocket star," blues and R&B singers and songwriters, actress, firefighter, ninja turtle, power rangers, teachers, musicians, rappers, Zorro, hair stylists, scientist, entrepreneurs, activists, you name it. Beautiful children with beautiful dreams. But dreams can become nightmares when a child lives in a household where there is domestic abuse and violence, even when they are not physically abused themselves.

The Centers for Disease Control and Prevention reports "in homes where violence between partners occurs, there is a 45% to 60% chance of co-occurring child abuse, a rate of 15 times higher than the average. Even when they are not physically attacked, children witness 68% to 80% of domestic assaults" (Edwards LMFT, 2019). Whatever is done to you is, by default, also done to your children.

When children are between the ages of a newborn and five years old, they receive all the information that will govern how they think, feel, react. They learn what is socially acceptable behavior in their family of origin and in the society around them. They are little sponges, absorbing our attitudes, thought processes, and actions. Their parents are their idols who, they think, know everything. A child in those formative years will internalize everything. If daddy is beating on mommy, children question whether or not they will be daddy's next victim. If a parent lashes out at their partner, calling him or her names or characterizing the other parent in a negative way, children may begin to believe and internalize what the negative parent says. An innocent child can unwittingly become a part of a gaslighting campaign.

As the child's psyche is developing, they begin to question themselves. Maybe mommy wouldn't get so mad if I got better grades, was quieter, a good girl, smarter. Daddy left because I wasn't good enough. If I were perfect, I would be loved.

At three years old, Ryan had processed and internalized information from studying his father. Watching his dad bark orders and the entire household jumping to comply, he asked, "Mommy, do you have to obey daddy too?" His father was standing there, proudly observing that his son knew who was "boss."

Ryan was a sweet, highly intelligent, inquisitive little boy. He was rarely on the receiving end of his father's rage. He adored Peter and, early on, began exhibiting signs of his father's negative behaviors. He learned that daddy was the head of household. He was beginning to believe that uncontrollable rage, subjugation of women, and disrespect were appropriate behavior, and that women were to obey and serve. Didn't everybody do what daddy said? Didn't daddy demand and get respect? Didn't mommy and everyone else fear him? His father taught him to "take the pain" and "men don't cry." He learned to be tough and reckless with his attitudes and behavior. When he purposely shoved his sister off the top of her bunk bed onto the hard wood floor, his dad said "Don't do it again." No further consequences or discipline. His father told his sister to get up off the floor, stop crying, and "You're alright." When Ryan fought with his sisters, they were often the ones who got into trouble and received his punishment. When we left and lived in a shelter, Ryan threw a little girl off the top of the sliding board to the ground. She was in his way. He was four years old when we left his dad. Neither he nor his elder brothers had escaped my husband's overly aggressive influence, especially regarding females. Ryan had absorbed it all and like most little boys, he wanted to be just like his dad. Tough, talented, admired, and feared.

Long after I left, the seeds of my abusive marriage continued to produce 10-fold in my children. I was devastated and afraid. Had I waited too long? How much damage had I done by not ending the relationship sooner? What could I do to turn things around? How could I turn me around? How would I undo all of the damage?

When we left, the younger children thought we were going on an adventure. My children often traveled with me. Only the oldest two knew we were running away. After about a month, Ryan began to worry about his father. Every day he asked if his father was dead. was so tiny that at four years old I was still carrying him on my hip. I couldn't tell him that his father was a dangerous man. I couldn't break my little boy's heart. I told him his father was sick and we needed to be away from him for a while so he could get well.

It is a myth that children are not affected by your partner's abusive behavior towards you. A child's narrative can be manipulated by a narcissistic parent against another parent, a sibling, or him or herself. A parent who beats or berates their partner in front of their children, then denies anything like that ever happened, is gaslighting the child by negating the child's reality. The child who experiences domestic violence, whether to himself or the victimized parent, internalizes it, learning to hate and blame themselves. When a child sees one parent abuse the other, they can feel helpless, abandoned, unsafe, and unprotected. A child who is gaslighted by a parent, used in the parent's campaign to undermine the partner, can feel that adults cannot be trusted. Children who experience gaslighting tend to hide who they are in order to receive love from the offending parent. Because of this, many children struggle with depression and other psychological issues they cannot talk about or explain, especially if this abuse happens in those formative years. This psychological attack will play out in unexplained behaviors like temper tantrums, rage, isolation, and self-harm. You are asking why they are acting out and they can't explain it. They have internalized their rage and fear which comes out as depression, anxiety, clinginess, misbehaving, drinking, fighting, using drugs.

Parents who have experienced trauma in their lives may try to control the narrative of their child's life out of fear. They don't want the child to experience the negative things that have happened to them. They want better for their children than the lives they had or the mistakes they made. They become helicopter parents or indulgent parents because of this desire for their children to be alright, to have it better, to not suffer as they did. This is normal behavior based on the circumstances but may cause the child to feel pressured to be perfect. A child needs balance, not lack of boundaries or too many strict rules. You can't change what happened by setting standards that the child finds impossible or improbable to reach. Eventually the child will rebel. You can't make up for what the offending parent did by giving in to a child's every whim, temper tantrums, and childhood rages.

Children don't come with manuals or warning labels. As parents who love and care about their children, we fudge it and do the best we can. But parents who have narcissistic personalities try to control the narrative to make themselves look good, often using a child as the scapegoat for their bad behavior or props to make it look like they are respectable, moral, virtuous, prosperous, and upright individuals. How many horror stories have we seen and heard of parents whose families appear wholesome in public, only to learn that their children have been physically or sexually abused and mistreated.

Narcissistic parents may pit one child against the other, or their children against a group of people. Whatever it takes to make the parent the hero. Older children can take sides based on what they understand or misunderstand. Children can also resent feeling like they need to protect you and/or take care of you. A child's brain can also be affected when witnessing abuse. Continuous exposure can change their neurological patterns and responses. When a child grows up living on survival, in fight or flight stage over an extended period of time, the endocrine system becomes imbalanced. The flight or fight response is highly developed in children exposed to domestic violence. Young children can develop extreme behaviors due to the amount of cortisol and adrenaline released into the brain during domestic violence episodes including but not limited to arguments, belittling behavior, and assault. This unbalanced hormonal activity influences a child's capacity to learn, to regulate his or her actions and emotions including fear and anger, or to manage feeling overwhelmed. Domestic violence is a negative hack on a child's central nervous system. This early exposure to trauma can lead to lifelong physical, emotional, sexual, and psychological health problems.

Sadly, parents are not the only ones who can gaslight, bully, or abuse children. Teachers can gaslight their students by publicly shaming them, calling a child dumb, not as smart as Suzy or Billy, asking questions like "Where are your brains?" Ryan had a second-grade teacher who cursed at her students, called them names, threatened them with abuse, and intimidated them with threats of repercussions if they told their parents about how she talked to and treated them. Most of the children were terrified. My son and two or three other students told their parents. After confronting the teacher and, I admit, threatening her should she harm my son and any other student in any way, shape, or form, I went to the principal. To my surprise, there were two other parents joining me. We had all heard the same things from our children. The principal told us another parent had previously reported on this same teacher. We asked what the principal had done. She said she had spoken with the teacher and that was it. The three of us demanded the teacher be fired. Two of us let the principal know that if the matter wasn't settled, we would take it to the school board and request that both teacher and principal be fired. The teacher was fired by week's end.

Child abuse can also happen in places of worship where spiritual leadership is regarded as truth tellers and children, or their victimized parent made a liar. Spiritual leaders can mislead a congregation by gaslighting as in cases like Jim Jones, the renowned cult leader who terrorized and beat children while their parents watched, pit spouses and children against each other, raped young girls and boys he was attracted to, and led a massacre by poison. The children were injected with the poison first, babies given syringes of cyanide squirted down their throats.

Has your child ever felt the need to insert himself verbally or physically between you and your spouse, partner, or significant other to stop an argument or protect you from a fight? Has your child ever witnessed domestic violence whether verbal, physical, sexual, economic, or social? Have you had to escape with your children to be safe? Has your child ever been caught in the crossfire of you and your partner's arguments, sustaining any type of physical or emotional harm? Is your child easily frightened, startled, or having recurring nightmares? Is he or she fatigued, moody, unusually quiet and reserved? Is your child self-isolating, showing signs of depression, self-loathing, wetting the bed? How are your child's grades in school?

As a parent, you can help your child by genuinely listening to your children's fears without judging them or getting defensive. Maintain neutral ground. Don't pressure your child to talk. The goal is to let them know you are there for them and they can talk if and when they want to, even if it's not to you.

Get your children the help they will need through psychological counseling, connection with community organizations and resources, and other outlets for their energy and anger. Get them involved in sports, art, book clubs, dance, theater, or other extracurricular activities they may be interested in. They need a place where they can feel safe and free to express themselves. Be as consistent as possible with their chosen activity.

Your child may withdraw from their normal friendships and cultivate more destructive associations. He or she may act out violently, have dramatic drop in grades at school, become anti-social. Be conscious of these behaviors. They are warning signs that something is wrong. Your children may be having a tough time even when the abuse has not extended to them. Be consistent and clear about what behaviors are acceptable and which are not. Be compassionate and firm without blaming your child for what has or is happening to him or her. It can get pretty tough for the both of you, especially in the case of the very young who cannot articulate for themselves, and teenagers who can become very moody, withdrawn, and self-destructive.

If you don't have children and abuse is not your story, you can create a safe space for your niece, nephew, or neighborhood child where they can feel accepted and at home. A place where children feel they can be themselves. A place of peace rather than violence in tone or behavior. A place where they feel heard.

In a domestic violence situation, children are often casualties. One of the best ways to keep them safe is to take care of yourself as best you can. Your children need you. They are concerned for you, whether or not the abuse has extended to them. You too must find ways to connect with your community, find activities that give you joy and peace, create a safe space for yourself and a safety plan for you and your children. (See Safety Planning in the Resources page at the end of this book.)

We want what is best for our children. We want to keep them safe and out of harm's way. To do this, we must be conscious that they too are suffering. It is not their fault. They are the innocents, whether infants, toddlers, grade school or teens. I did not want to take my children away from everything they knew and everyone they loved. I thought they were living in a happy bubble. I didn't know they knew what was happening to me. I weighed leaving in the balance for quite some time because I didn't want to drastically disrupt their lives. How could I keep them safe? I had an excellent job, contract work teaching dance and drama classes. I got paid pretty well for it, could take my children to work with me, and enjoyed my work. What would I do to make a living if I left? How would I take care of them? Then the abuse began extending to them. Like most women in my shoes, my children were the reason I stayed and the reason I left. When I left, I held on with both hands through homelessness and economic hardship because of my children. I refused to give up even when I wanted to end it all because I knew I had mouths to feed and hearts in need of healing. My children saved me. The journey was immensely difficult, but in saving them, I found myself, my strength, my courage, my tenacity. They were my insurance against quitting when times got extraordinarily tough. They were my lifelines when I needed a laugh or a hug. It took some time after the fallout, but we operated as one unit.

As a parent, your children need you to be at your best. They do not need you to be perfect, have all the answers, or get everything right. They need you. More than the money you spend on things to keep them occupied, more than the time you spend trying to get everything in the perfect order at the perfect time, more than any other example you can give them, they need you to be alright. They need you to ditch the guilt you may feel and make a move on their behalf, even if you and they at first struggle with the consequences of that move. They need you to be free so they can be free. Your children need you to be strong, loving, and patient with them. They need you to be a fighter, a warrior for your peace so they can have peace. They need to see you laughing and having fun. They need to see you happy and at the top of your game. They need to see by example that they too can overcome a difficult situation. You are their lifeline. The greatest blessing you can give a child living with domestic violence is to recover yourself so you can recover all.

Teens and Dating Violence

It takes courage to grow up and become who you really are. – E. E. Cummings

Growing up is challenging work. From the first time your baby rolls over and sits up, you are supporting its progress, reporting every milestone to the doctor and anyone else who will listen and watch with you. As your baby crawls across the floor, you watch to make sure he or she isn't picking up something dreadful and putting it in his mouth. When they began that slow toddle, stand-step-crouch-fall, finding their legs, you proudly clap and encourage them to grow. Then they do, becoming school age, preteens, and teenagers. Your worries that they might pick up something that will harm them increase 100-fold.

It is challenging and confusing in this day and age to be a child. Natural curiosity about body parts and how they function, developing friendships, cultivating personal interests are all a normal part of a child's growth and development. The flood of hormones raging through the body, middle school and high school courses and exams, pressure from parents and teachers to fall in line with structure, and pressure from peers to rebel can make the pre-teen and teen years confusing and tumultuous. In the 21st century, the added pressure of social media and instant snapshots of a child's life can play an even more complicated role in their growth and development.

Peer pressure now includes cyber bullying, internet stalking, and receiving unwanted sexual advances through text and phone messages. According to an article in the Washington Post published in 2019, explicit text messages between teens and preteens is a common practice with 14.8% of kids ages 12-17 having sent explicit text messages and 24.8% receiving them (Pahr, 2019).

Beyond a child's natural curiosity, there is a heightened sexual presence on internet streaming and gaming channels even for children as young as seven and eight years old. Some seemingly innocent internet sites are actually trafficking sites for pedophiles and those who sell children for labor and sex. From the 60's to the 90's children, pre-teens, and teens explored their sexuality and friendships with the mentality, "you show me yours; I'll show you mine." The advent of modern technologies has created a virtual minefield for teens and their sexual interactions. Sexting is a criminal offense and for the unwary teen boy who sends his partner a penis pic or the unwary girl who sends her partner a pic of her private parts, a jail sentence can be attached with a hefty fine and a "sex offender" label that follows them for life. Long before they are fully psychologically developed, their innocent "I'll show you mine" can land them in court. Normal curiosity about sexuality and how the body functions at this time in their lives is often complicated by laws that can have a twelve year old locked up for being curious and a 17 year old categorized as a sexual offender for sending nude photos to his girlfriend, even if it is at her request.

Teen dating violence is also of critical concern for parents and their young people navigating social interactions in a social media world. In their study of over 1,000 teens, the National Institute of Justice recognized that teen dating violence is often a precursor to adult domestic violence. This study highlights the need for more conversations and assistance for young people in their teen and pre-teen years so they understand what dating violence looks like, what love is and is not, and how to establish boundaries in real life and on social media. NIJ Principal Investigator Peggy Giordano stated, "It actually would be important to get a start early as they're navigating these relationships and try to interrupt these processes before they become chronic or firmly entrenched" (Mulford, Ph.D. & Giordano, Ph.D., 2008).

The Center for Disease Control and Prevention Youth Risk Behavior Survey and data from the National Intimate Partner and Sexual Violence Survey report that "26% of women and 15% of men who were victims of contact sexual violence, physical violence, and/or stalking by an intimate partner in their lifetime first experienced these or other forms of violence by that partner before age eighteen with the median age between twelve and seventeen"(National Center for Injury Prevention and Control & Division of Violence Prevention, 2019).

Dating violence can now occur in an online and texting minefield. An angry teenaged boyfriend, jilted by his girl, can post nude photos of her online to shame her. Employers may see these photos causing the end of her chosen career before it starts. A jealous teen can out his gay partner on social media without the partner's consent. Sending unwanted lewd text messages, threats, texted psychological abuse, sextortion, and gaslighting can now occur online and off. Pre-teens and teens are very social beings spending 70 to 90 percent of their time online and on their cell phones or tablets leaving them more exposed to this new type of predatory violence.

Most teens and pre-teens do not report violence, including sexual assault. If they come from an abusive background, they may view the behavior as normal and even acceptable. They are more likely to also blame themselves and feel ashamed. Children and youth at higher risk of dating violence are those who come from abusive households, are mistreated in foster care systems, or are exposed early to a "pathway of violence" including caregivers "exposing or involving the child [pre-adolescence] in illegal activity or other activities that may foster delinquency or antisocial behavior [which] is a consistent predictor of a higher likelihood that those adolescents would later become victims of dating violence" (National Institute of Justice). Only about 33% of teens in abusive relationships ever talk or tell anyone about what is happening to them (One Love Foundation, 2020). Violence in adolescent relationships can set the stage for intimate partner and sexual violence in the future and for the rest of the perpetrator and victim's adult life. It is critical that these things are addressed as early as possible.

It is critical that young people and their parents learn skills necessary to develop healthy relationships. Ending relationship violence in young people depends on teaching young adults about what abusive behaviors are and what they look like. Some young perpetrators are adept at appearing like the guy or girl next door, manipulating parents and friends of the person being abused. It is important that parents are aware of the signs and signals of dating violence which includes but is not limited to:

- Hitting, kicking, pushing, pulling hair, biting, or other physical harm. If you see bruises on your child, ask questions. Approach the subject gently. Let your child know they can talk to you about anything.
- Threatening, name calling, insulting, cyber bullying. This may not happen in front of you. If your child is suddenly depressed, anxious, or afraid, it is time to ask questions.
- Forcing a partner to take part in a sex act. If your outgoing child begins to socially isolate, or your introvert child becomes more closed mouth, you may need to seek help. Offer information so that if the child doesn't want to talk to you, at least at first, they can talk to someone and get help. Loveisrespect.org offers a 24-hour hotline, 1-866-331-9474, and a 24-hour text, 22522. Thetrevorproject.org for LGBTQ youth offers a 24-hour hotline, 1-866-488-7386 and a 24-hour text; text Start to 678678.
- Unwanted phone calls, text messages, or showing up unannounced and unwanted.

- Repeated texting in order to annoy, aggravate, or cause psychological harm.
- Posting sexual pictures online without permission.
- Outing a person online, to his parents, friends, or relatives without permission.

Teen dating violence is preventable. Communication and education is key to helping young people recognize and navigate healthy relationships. The more social support children and youth have, the less dating violence occurs. It is important that young people and their parents learn about what constitutes healthy relationships. Some characteristics of healthy relationships include:

- Open, effective, non-violent communication. This includes productive disagreement and conflict resolution skills. This also includes effective listening and speaking. When a child feels they can communicate with you openly, they are more likely to come to you when there is trouble.
- Managing emotions.
- Interactions based on respect, love, and trust even when partners like different things or see things differently.
- Demonstrated positive family dynamics. Strong, supportive families including extended family based on love, respect, and honoring one another's differences.
- Community engagement and support including mentorship, community activities like sports and theatre, and support groups.
- Social media training and transparency. A 13-year-old can have a social media account if their parent signs for it. An astute child can get around the parent permissions. Teach your child about safe and appropriate social media interaction before exposing them to the media minefield.

- Interpersonal skills including negotiation, empathy, compassion, leadership, collaboration, and awareness.
- Personal development including the importance of self-awareness, self-esteem, problem-solving skills, goal setting and achievement.

Both male and female youth need help to process and deal with the consequences of dating violence. The repercussions include depression, anxiety, isolation, and physical health challenges which can follow young people into adulthood. The more social support children and youth have, the less dating violence occurs. For more information on how to help teens, see Resources for Young Adults, Teens, and Tweens at the back of this book.

6 *CHAPTER SIX*

<u>Losing God</u>

It was even harder to live with the idea that things happened to people for no reason, that God had lost touch with the world and nobody was in the driver's seat. — Harold S. Kushner

My six siblings and I grew up with a mom who was extremely strict about our religious upbringing. We attended a Pentecostal church all day Sunday, Monday for YPHA meetings, Tuesday for prayer meeting, Wednesday for mid-week service, Thursday for choir rehearsal. We may have had Friday off, but Saturday was also rehearsal and cleaning the church with my grandfather who was a trustee. Holidays there was more church. If attendance was the prerequisite for holiness, we were one of the holiest families alive.

I had become a student of the Bible at age 13, studying the scriptures historically, literally, and as metaphor. At around age fifteen, regardless of all my devout upbringing, I lost God for the first time. I did not understand or agree with the theology of the Pentecostal doctrine with all its rules and regulations. From my teenage viewpoint, God was an angry father scowling down from his throne in heaven, judging everything I said and did. I debated with ministers and teachers concerning sectarianism, what passed for rules of modesty for women, and eschewing dance and theatre, the two things I was most interested in. I argued about the foolishness of the rule that women should not wear pants based on the scripture in Deuteronomy 22:5. I argued that pants were not worn by anyone in those days so how could it apply. I also debated the no dancing rule, postulating that it didn't make sense in light of the fact that King David was said to have danced out of his clothes.

My grandmother told my mother I was an old soul. I knew things I shouldn't have known as a child and could see things long before they ever happened. At fifteen, I had not heard that "still small voice" that grown folk talked about, nor had I seen God in the way they claimed. But there was a knowing in me that I could not explain. As a result, my constant questioning and ability to debate well, which I saw as no different than Jesus in the temple at age 12, had me courteously ushered out of my Sunday school class and transported to the adult class which I found horribly boring. I spent one or two weeks there and then began teaching the pre-school and kindergarten children's class which I thoroughly enjoyed.

I realize what I had truly lost was the belief in systems that I felt made women and girls less than boys and men. I had lost the indoctrination of beliefs that kept me bound to a certain way of living, feeling, and being.

I lost God again in my twenties. I questioned his existence, challenging him to show himself if he was real. Moses did the same thing as a young man when he was leading the people of Israel. He no more understood who Spirit was than any of us in the wilderness of our lives. I needed God to prove himself to me. I felt like there was more to this mythical, mystical being than met the eye and I wanted to know for sure who he, she, or it was. In answer, I heard that still, small voice. I felt the gentle presence of a being that never shouted, attacked, scolded, or scorned. I once heard Spirit say clearly, "Get up!" when I was laying around feeling sorry for myself. The words were spoken so firmly I jumped off the couch looking to see if someone had entered the room. I learned to pay attention.

Throughout my life, God and I have played hide-and-seek, with me doing most of the hiding. I have closed my ears to the voice of Spirit, lost my faith, and had the foundations of my beliefs horribly shaken. Whether fearful, angry, sad, or arrogant, and even in my well place, I have ignored and discounted the presence of a supreme being who "sat high and looked low" as the elders in my church used to say. I have been confused by the God lauded as healer and deliverer who allowed destruction and harm. I have been reluctant to believe in Jesus as God incarnate. I have questioned everything and from it I have learned that omnipotence is not afraid of questions and, when asked, will reveal the answers. I realized the more I followed the traditions of men, the more my path blurred. I have found that if you live long enough, you will get to a place where you lose the God of your social circle and ecumenical upbringing and find out what you really believe about the creator and the universe.

I have heard people say, "God took your child because heaven needed another angel," and "Your child (or any loved one) probably died to show you that you need to get your life together." I have had someone say to me that the reason I have an incurable neuro disease is because I was being hard-headed, and God wants me to sit down and listen to him. I was told that if I repent, if I forgive, if I do x, y, and z, I will be healed. I heard the same rhetoric when I lived with my abusive husband. If you would just get right, do right, be right, everything will be all right.

God created all the angels he needed from the beginning of time. Evil and good exists in a world we humans control, one in which God rarely intervenes as he has given us authority over all of this mess we have created. The reality is life happens without rhyme or reason. Sometimes things do not make any sense. Illness can come suddenly from anywhere at any time. Healthy men drop dead. Innocent children die, disappear, and are sex trafficked. Sometimes things don't make sense. Yes, there are occasions when our bad decisions put us in positions that later grieve our souls and cause others pain. We have to take responsibility for that. We must also know that rain still falls on the just and the unjust, the humble and the proud, the wretched and the opulent, the wicked and the holy man. No matter how good we think we are, how many good deeds we do, how passionately we serve, we are not exempt from tragedy or trauma.

Rabbi Harold S. Kushner lost his fifteen year old son to a tragic neuro disease. He said useless platitudes were, "*comforting the way the religion of Job's friends was comforting: it worked only as long as we did not take the problems of innocent victims seriously. When we have met Job, when we have been Job, we cannot believe in that sort of God any longer without giving up our own right to feel angry, to feel that we have been treated badly by life...if we can bring ourselves to acknowledge that there are some things God does not control, many good things become possible*" (Kushner, 1981, pgs. 50-51).

Because I lost the traditional God of rituals, laws, and doctrine that kept me bound, I found the vastness and greatness of my source, the universe, and the God consciousness inside of me. Although some of my early beliefs about God are foundational to who I am as a spiritual being, there are those weights that I have left by the wayside in order to get close to the light of my purpose and power on this planet and in this world. Each time I have lost God, I have been rebuilt, renewed, restored. There were some old ideas that I had to discard because they no longer applied to the journey I was on. Some things I had to wrestle with. Like

Job, I questioned my suffering and the suffering of others in the world – the destitute and dispossessed, needy and at risk children, abused women and the disparity in justice and equality for them and their children. I have had to give up the notion that God can and will fix everything if we pray loud, long, and hard enough. I had to give up the idea that if I am a good girl, good things will happen to me. Terrible things happen to good people all day long every day.

I had to give up the idea that God is in control of everything, and everything happens for a reason. I had to strip power from the belief that there is an omniscient devil, more powerful than God, who can negate all of heaven's promises. I have learned that much of the evil we see here on planet earth is due to the evil present in man. I have visually, with my normal vision, seen demonic spirits attached to others, influencing their decisions. I have learned that spiritual beings are no respecter of persons and both spiritual and natural laws apply to us all. Gravity and the changing of seasons, hot and cold, living on earth in heaven or hell. I have accepted and embraced all of this. Losing God helped me to come face to face with the reality that there is more to the master of the universe than what meets the eye.

In Egyptian history, there was a discussion of whether there was one God or many gods. The God Ra, represented by the sun, was the supreme God. Native Americans believed God or Spirit exists in many forms, especially in nature. Africans have had a strong connection to Spirit with the belief that one can be inhabited by a spirit, whether divine or evil. All of these traditions have commonalities. Whether you believe in one supreme God or many, whether you call that divine presence Allah, God, Ra, Source, Infinite Intelligence, or Spirit, history tells us plainly that the secrets of the universe unfold in layers peeled back over time, a beautiful, bountiful mystery.

Losing my traditional beliefs about God caused me to see things in a much wider scope than the tunnel vision I had become accustomed to. When I lost God, when I lost other people's perception of God, when I lost what I once believed, I came to a broader and deeper understanding that God, the Universe, Source, and I are one. I have come to know that thing called God-consciousness, the thing Jesus himself spoke of when he said, "I and the father are one" (John 10:30 KJV).

Because God and I are one, because we are related and inseparable as mother is to child and father is to son, I have been endowed with the same creative power. I have the same ability to transform and change, the same ability to speak life, the same ability to resurrect and be resurrected. The writer of Psalm 82:5,6 says:

"They know not, neither will they understand; they walk in darkness: all the foundations of the earth are out of course. I have said ye are gods; and all of you are children of the most high."

John 10:34-38, Jesus speaking to the Pharisees argues that scripture (law) which "cannot be set aside" says "ye are gods" so why do you have trouble with me calling myself the son of God and saying that I and the father are one. In essence, Jesus was saying "I'm agreeing with your law so why are you so offended?"

There are going to be some blows in your life, some minimal, some fatal. Accept that. Life is going to happen. But ye are gods. Little gods living a human experience on earth. You are the children of a most high being thus endowed with incredible strength and resourcefulness. Everything is yours. You must learn how to access it. To speak those things that be not as though they were and put the work in. Nothing is guaranteed. Everything is a faith walk. Sometimes you will lose which does not mean you have no faith. It means that you will have to strengthen what remains and stay the course on life's incalculable journey.

I am grateful for the opportunity to live this adventure and to spend my life in helping others navigate the journey to recovering themselves. When I feel lost and alone, mother nature always brings me back into the presence of my source. I willingly follow her gaze from the shoreline or when I look upon a sunrise. I see her when I am surprised by a bright red cardinal perched on a tree limb watching me, or a grasshopper sitting still at my feet. She always guides me into the very presence and atmosphere of heaven in all its glory and Spirit in all its form. My perfect parents, Mother Nature and Father God, never leave me nor forsake me. No matter how often I lose them, Spirit is always with me.

In losing God, I have learned to gather as much light, joy, and peace as I can so that I and others can be illuminated as we walk along the way. Losing my former concepts of God, I have gained a greater understanding of my place, purpose, and connection to the universe. Developing a God consciousness, the belief that God resides without and within, is a paradigm that I can live by and live out on a daily basis. In losing God, every time, I found answers to questions I had not been bold enough, courageous enough, or aware enough to ask. In losing the God of my fathers, I found a God of my own.

Transformation or Transmission

If you don't transform your suffering...you will transmit your suffering to your family, your neighbors, even to your country.- Father Richard Rohr

I think I have always believed in the old adage that if you are not growing, you are dying. I am a student of the universe. My entire life has been about learning and growing. About asking questions and researching answers. I was one of those precocious children who needed to know why the sky is blue and the grass green. I have spent my life on a quest to continually move forward by growing and learning.

One of the things I have learned along this adventure of life is the most loving thing I could have done for my marriage, for my children, even for my community was to leave my husband Peter. I had to take us both out of a situation where we would continue to harm our children and one another.

Over the years, I had become self-destructive, not caring whether he killed me or not, even hoping he would, to put an end to all the threats. Like a hand grenade whose pin had been plucked and ammo thrown, I came to a place in my heart and head where I knew I would do irreparable harm to Pete the next time he attempted to hurt me or our children. My then 15-year-old son, who had once loved and admired his stepfather, now hated him with such vengeance he was seeking a gun to do what he always believed he was supposed to do, protect his family. My then 14-year-old daughter was breaking down, developing unhealthy relationships, contending with suicidal ideation, and racing down her own path of self-destruction. My then eight year old daughter, who had loved and idolized her stepfather, was now afraid of him. One day he had tried to wipe her face with a rag full of paint after she and her five-year-old little sister had accidently spilled some on the linoleum kitchen floor.

I had been planning our escape for a year when my eldest daughter came into my room screaming and crying, her mouth full of accusations. "You said to NEVER let anyone treat you like this! Why are you just sitting there! Why are you taking that from him! Why aren't you doing something? Why are you not doing anything?"

She had heard Peter yelling at me, calling me names, cursing at me, throwing things. She didn't know about the plan. I couldn't tell her. She was a child. I wanted to calm her, to reassure her, but I was afraid of putting her in a more dangerous predicament. I was also afraid she would run away again if I didn't tell her and, instead of carrying out my plan, I would have to go looking for her which might delay our exit for months. So, against my better judgment, I told her I was leaving Peter, swearing her to secrecy. She told her brother who told their step-brother, Peter's son. Miraculously, word never got to Peter.

At one time, Peter had purchased a little burgundy car from his sister, claiming it was for the family. It was too small for the both of us and six children but then, it really wasn't for us. Peter would hide the keys or take the battery out of the car when he wasn't using it so I wouldn't be able to drive it. It was a game he bragged about to his sister. Then, with our income tax money, he purchased a ten passenger van that smoked like a chimney and wouldn't start at the wholesale dealership where we purchased it. I was not a fan. My protests fell on deaf ears. He drove the van to work where it would sit for 12 hours a day while the children and I walked or took the bus, no matter the weather. The burgundy car disappeared. He said it had been towed away. Months later I saw the car, with its definite markings, at my mother's church. She said it belonged to a young woman who attended. My wedding pearls, a gift from Peter, had disappeared at the same time as the car. I wondered if the young lady ever wore them to church.

With our next income tax, Peter purchased another vehicle, a sexy silver Park Avenue. I wasn't allowed to drive the van, also in his sister's name, until two men from the church got on Peter about making me and the children walk when there were two vehicles. His excuse was that I did not have a license. I did. Peter did not know it at the time. His license, unknown to me, had been suspended. He had been driving on a suspended since before he and I were married. That's why everything was in his sister's name. The two gentlemen, whose wives had told them, let Peter know that I did indeed have a driver's license.

When I was finally allowed to drive the van, Peter got it illegally inspected. The police officer who pulled me over was nice enough to explain to me, as he scraped the sticker off my windshield, that Pennsylvania inspection stickers were not brown. As the officer was talking, I had an immediate flashback of the argument Peter and I had concerning how the smoking van could have passed inspection.

There are two main reason we hear the ticking of a clock in our lives. It is either a timer or a bomb. Peter blamed me for the inspection sticker debacle. He warned me that he would take the van and let me and the children walk again since I was so "unappreciative and irresponsible." I heard the tick, tick when I opened his palm, dropped the keys in his hand, and walked away. Taking the vehicle whose tags could be traced was not a part of the plan. I was nothing if not strategic.

Peter came home while our escape was in motion. Our driver, we'll call him Joe, had a small vehicle, and could only fit the two eldest and their luggage in his car. They went to the Greyhound station first. Joe got lost getting to the station which threw our timing way off. Ryan, Tina, and Tasha (not her real name) had fallen asleep on the couch. Ryan woke up suddenly. He raised himself up and said in a groggy sing song voice, "Daddy's coming," then went right back to sleep. I stood completely still in shocked silence for a few seconds. I knew my son's drowsy message was a premonition, a warning. Panicked, I grabbed the rest of the luggage, ran upstairs, and threw it way in the back of my spacious closet, covering it with dresses and other clothing items. Peter, who worked on an assembly line, wasn't supposed to leave work. He came home unexpectedly just as my youngest had predicted.

I had no way of warning Joe who, by this time, had dropped the two eldest off at the station and was on his way back. I struggled remaining calm and praying the children would stay asleep and Joe's arrival would be delayed. Peter looked around the house and asked questions. He told me he was taking the van to the shop to get it properly inspected. He said he would be back after he dropped it off. I did not know how much time that would buy me.

Immediately after Peter left, I sounded the alarm. I called everyone who was a part of the plan. I worried. If things went south and Peter found out I was leaving him, it was going to be bad. Really bad. I was terrified.

I called Joe and asked how far away he was. He was fifteen minutes out. When he got to the house, I didn't worry about a car seat for my youngest or anything else. I threw in what luggage I could and left the rest. In my hurry, I forgot to get the food I had prepared for the journey. I had about $20.00 in cash and some snacks that I had shoved into some of the children's book bags. Two pieces of luggage, five book bags, the kids' favorite stuffed animals, and the clothes on our backs. That's what we left with.

We spent eight hours on that Greyhound bus, not including the two or three rest stops that we made along the way. The bus had to go past our house first. The two eldest and I ducked down in case Peter was around and saw us. The police stopped the bus several miles out. My heart almost jumped out of my chest thinking Peter had found out and got the police to come get me. I was afraid he had used the police to come take my two youngest children, his children, as he had threatened many times. He was their biological father and the lawyers had already told me it was illegal to cross state lines with them without Peter's approval.

They claimed my children were a ward of the state. I responded that the state did not open its legs and push out those children. That was all me. I was also told that I would have to sit down and mediate with my husband, the man who had threatened to kill me. To me, that was not an option. Who mediates with a madman?

I loved my husband when I left him. Some people think that's crazy. How can you love someone who mistreats you, abuses you, and harms you on purpose? I loved his potential. I still loved what I had first seen in him, the great man I knew he could be. I waited for years for the man I fell in love with to reappear. The man who was smart, romantic, generous, funny, deeply spiritual, caring, compassionate, and sexy. I missed that guy. Even after I left him, I still hoped that we could one day reconcile our differences and get it right.

Living in an atmosphere of abuse and negativity will change you. There is no doubt about that. As Peter became increasingly violent in word and deed toward me, I began reciprocating in kind.

On the rare occasions we went out, Peter always took me to upscale restaurants. One evening while having dinner at one of these places, he began yelling at me and calling me names. The restaurant was crowded. Every table was occupied. I was humiliated and embarrassed as people looked on, whispering behind cloth napkins, and shaking their heads. I said nothing. Peter returned to his meal and suddenly began choking on a shrimp. I watched as the color drained from his face. He started turning blue. I sat silently, calmly, watching. I was a certified fitness trainer. I knew how to do the Heimlich and CPR. I did nothing. I said nothing. I sat emotionless and still, watching, my hands in my lap. It occurred to me in that moment that I could sit and watch this man die feeling oddly vindicated. Staring at him, one side of my mouth turned upward a little at the thought.

Peter got his breath back, his choking relieved as suddenly as it had come upon him. I ate with glee. Peter watched me warily the rest of the evening. Neither of us spoke a word.

That night I realized I was becoming someone else. Something evil was stirring inside of me. I knew, eventually, I too would be capable of doing him harm with no remorse.

I left more for my children than I did for myself. They were my priority. I didn't want my sons to believe that calling a woman names, withholding affection, threatening and so on was acceptable behavior. I didn't want my daughters to believe that women were inferior, and it was okay to treat them as such. I wanted more for them and thus I will never regret my leaving. NEVER!

Leaving had a cost. I couldn't prevent the scarring my children had already received. I watched three of them, a son and two daughters, go through abusive relationships. I saw the effects on all five children in various areas of their life and in various stages. It was disheartening. I had made the leap, but I had not transformed my suffering. My husband and I had transmitted it to our children. This was a heartbreaking realization. I blamed myself. I had stayed too long. They had seen and experienced too much. It was all on me or so I thought at the time.

Transformation is the ability to turn one thing into something else. To turn pain into power. To turn struggle into strength, frustration into freedom and dark nights into daylight. To turn hatred into compassion and love into light. It took me more than a decade of work on myself to transform. It is the work I will be doing for the rest of my life. What I learned is that you can make a choice at any time to change. You can make a choice to do better. You can choose to see things from the other side. When I stopped blaming myself, when I forgave myself, I began to see things from another perspective. The more I worked on myself, the more I saw the beauty in the intricate tapestry of my experience.

My eldest daughter said to me one day, "Mom, I didn't know who you really were until we left. Before that I only saw you as mom and Mr. Peter's wife." That was an "aha" moment for me. I didn't get to become me again until I moved to a place where no one knew me, and I could fully be myself. No mask. No pretending. No faking it. The real me showed up in Virginia and I fell in love with her. I took her dancing on the beach every morning and watched the sun rise. I laughed more, smiled more, and fought harder, exercising faith in ways I could not have imagined existed outside of where I had been.

Change is a choice and when we talk about transformation, we are talking about making tough decisions that will feel gravely uncomfortable. We are talking about letting go of blame and focusing on growth. We are talking about loving and letting go, facing our own hurts in order to heal them, and readjusting our focus to see beauty in the worst circumstances and situations.

Peter was not an animal. He was not a mean creature. He was a man who had issues he had not faced, hurts he had not healed, and demons he had not exorcised. Socialized by abuse and neglect in his formative years, Peter's demons were a result of transmission of generations of abuse. This does not in any way excuse his behavior. Peter had made his own choices. It is merely the other side of the looking glass. It was not my job to throw holy water on his demons or heal his pain. It was my choice to love him enough to leave him, to keep him safe from the wrath that was growing inside of me, and to cut the cord so that he and I could both go on.

It was also my choice to transform my life into something wonderful, beautiful, and new. To always remember the beauty in what we had. The long walks where we talked for hours about anything and everything. The first time he kissed me. The times we sang oldies together with the children. The entire family crowded together in our bedroom as we all watched his favorite movie, *The Temptations*, a video that the children and I had presented to him on Father's Day. The many times he had been a good father and a good man. I chose to remember the beauty, put the pain in perspective and use it to empower me and others. To be grateful for all that I learned along the way.

In doing the work of transformation, I've allowed my children to see the other side of struggle. I tell them, don't go through anything without getting something good out of it. No matter how hard you have to look to find it, get something good. That's the gift of transformation.

The honeymoon phase in an abusive relationship is an illusion. It is a lie. A magic trick we hold on to because it feels so good at the time, and we want it to remain. We believe with all of our hearts that this is a good person who is just making bad choices right now. We give them the benefit of the doubt until the day we hear the tick, tick, tick, which tells us something is about to explode. We know the sound of it even when all is quiet. We feel it. It is a knowing in our bones. We ignore it hoping that we are wrong, second guessing ourselves, telling ourselves that we are overanalyzing. Our master illusionist plays to our wants, needs, dreams and desires that we shared with him/her in the first romantic falling-in-love stages of our relationship. We pray and hope for the phase to remain, all the time knowing that the sun does not stay in the sky after dark.

You can't hide behind the honeymoon. Doing so will cause you to bequeath the insanity of walking on eggshells, accepting insidious behavior, and living a lie to your children and the next generation. Like an infectious disease it will spread, spilling out into your family, your community, your city, and the world. Nothing on this earth happens in a vacuum. What happened to our family affected our church, the young people I served in that church, our neighbors, community, family, and friends.

Abundant life, though always available, is not free. It will cost you something. There will inevitably come a day where you will have to choose between transformation and transmission. Only you get to decide what price you are willing to pay and what it's all worth to you. Transmission is transferal of a blessing or a curse. Transformation is giving birth to possibility. If you can get through the labor pains of transformation, you can give birth to a more loving, giving, compassionate self which will not only change you, but everyone who is a witness to the light you have become.

Gratitude

I don't have to chase extraordinary moments to find happiness — It's right in front of me if I'm paying attention and practicing gratitude. — Brene Brown

Gratitude is my superpower. So much so that I write about it every day. I have a gratefulness journal, a little hardbound notebook I bought from the dollar store. Writing in it is the first thing I do every morning. It's like saying a prayer, a meditation if you will. There are days I go back and read what I've written realizing that I am repeatedly grateful for some of the same things. I am grateful for my health. I am grateful I am able to see the sun rise and set every day. I am grateful I can breathe of my own volition. I am grateful I have not lost my mind.

The decision to leave an abusive relationship is an exceedingly difficult one. I prayed my husband and I could get it right, that God would intervene. There were times that the Spirit of God did step in and protect me and my children in ways small and great. There were also times I lived afraid. Times when life was tremendously problematic, strenuous, and exhausting. Nights long ago when, watching my children asleep, all six of us crowded into one hotel room, I knew the next day a park bench was a great possibility. I am grateful we survived. I am grateful for the character and compassion that was developed in my children. Something I did not see or comprehend until many years later. I am extremely grateful for all those who helped us get to a place of safety enabling us to survive and thrive.

I have learned to find the collateral beauty in all of the damage even when I have had to dig deep for it, crawl on my hands and knees, lay on my face through the darkness blinded in order to see it, grasp it, feel it, and live it. I confess, I do not pray much anymore, at least in the way and form I used to. More often I meditate, giving thanks and being mindful. This is a much more effective way of communicating with the Spirit for me. I rarely ask for anything. Mostly, I find things to be grateful for in present tense.

Living in a home where yelling, screaming, and threatening is the order of the day, where tyranny rules, you find absolutely nothing to be grateful for. You may find days you are grateful he did not hit you and days you wish he did just to get it over with. You find yourself confused about your own feelings and muddled in your mind. You love the person and hate them at the same time. Gratefulness is not on the agenda. It finds no place on the menu. Protecting yourself and those you love takes precedence.

When my children, cousins, nieces, and nephews were small, I shared a story with them about truth and happiness. One of my many mentors shared the story with me. The story begins with the creation of man. In the beginning man was genuinely happy and the devil did not like it. He and his minions got together and had a meeting to decide where to hide truth and happiness. The council of evil rejected hiding it in the highest mountain. Man was too curious. He would climb the mountain and find it. They rejected hiding it in the depths of the sea. Man was adventurous. He would dive to the depths just for fun and find it there. They rejected hiding it in the core of the earth. Man was courageous. He would dig to the center of the earth and find it there. The devil himself finally came up with a brilliant idea. He said, "We'll hide truth and happiness inside man. He will never look there."

We often seek validation from outside of ourselves. We tend to outsource our energy. Women especially give so much of themselves that there is truly little left. When our energy gets depleted, we find ourselves running on fumes. Blinded by the things that have happened to us, the pain we are in, the hurt we have experienced, we cannot see the power that is inherent within us. That is the trick. The ultimate deception.

What is outside of you is an illusion. The power inside is real. It vibrates at a frequency that the earth, Mother Nature, God, Spirit, Source understands and responds to. Gratefulness is a way of raising that vibration to a level that helps you regain your in-sight. In the midst of sorrow, trouble, pain, disease, heartache, a tenacious spirit of gratefulness will give you vision. It is a way to help you see what you have to work with and to strengthen what remains. Are you in your right mind today despite the chaos you may be living in? Can you think clearly enough to learn, strategize, plan? Do you have any faith at all? We are not talking move a mountain kind of faith. We are talking mustard seed. That is all you need to take that leap into the void.

Do not focus on the long haul. Plan. Pray only if you believe in the prayer you are speaking into heaven, otherwise it is a waste. Be honest. No pretending. There is nobody to impress. If you have a journal, gratefulness or otherwise, speak the truth. If you do not feel grateful for anything in the moment, do not be afraid to write that. Healing comes with honesty. If you do not feel like writing anything that day, then don't.

Creativity and resourcefulness are activated in honest appreciation. You bless, meaning empower, yourself when you search for things to be grateful for. When you are gratitude focused, your brain begins to work out solutions to problems. Inspiration and ideas come by way of being thankful. You draw resources to you.

Scientifically, gratefulness increases the levels of serotonin in the brain which in turn increases dopamine, the feel good stuff. Increased dopamine gives us the will to live and to fight another day. Being thankful naturally changes your body's energy flow and the way your brain functions. It changes the atmosphere within you and around you. You may not feel or see the shift but appreciation in the tiniest measure can bend the trajectory of your life and circumstance.

Having an attitude of gratitude does not mean you will stop feeling sad, angry, betrayed. Life can deal some brutally damaging blows. It is not about sugar coating what you are going through and pretending things are not happening to you. It is not about putting a smile on your face when you are really dying inside or engaging in fantasy thinking or pretending to be happy when you are not. Dismiss the thought of faking it till you feel it. Be realistic about your situation. You cannot wish away abusive behaviors or personalities. To get to gratefulness, you must first acknowledge and confront difficult things.

To be grateful in the midst of hell takes courage. No doubt about that. But problems have solutions. Examine your problems realistically. Many problems come disguised as challenges. Thus, you must find the courage to dig deep, to the core of yourself, find what is good that remains, and strengthen those things.

You do not have to keep a journal. You do not have to write a list. You do not have to worry about numbers. To find something to be grateful for when you are broken, when your life has been shattered, when you are being mentally and physically battered is extremely challenging so never force it. Do not lie about your emotions of the moment. Do recognize that everything in life is subject to change. When someone brings harm to you, they also bring harm to themselves. We are all connected. There may be less than six degrees of separation and karma knows the address of all those who mistreated you, hurt you, and caused you irreparable harm.

Today, I am thankful for every wound and battle scar that tells me I have lived an adventurous life and overcome many challenges. Those scars tell me about myself. They say that I am a champion, an overcomer. They have a story, one in which I am the hero because I faced down whatever tried to destroy me and I survived, leaving a legacy of empowerment for my children, grandchildren and generations.

Gratefulness is not my superpower because it sounds good. It is my morning meditation. It is the only way I know of praying, the way that is the easiest and makes the most sense for me. It is the only way I can accept and understand there is love in this universe, in this world for me. When I hear the birds in the morning, I awake with a new sense of belonging to something greater than myself. It has been discovered that their song is a call to let others know that they did not die in the night. They are still here. I too am still here, and I am thankful.

I am thankful for what I have learned about myself and about human nature. I am thankful for strength I didn't know I had, endurance I wasn't aware of, and the love and kindness that has surrounded and supported me through the years. I am grateful to still be in the land of the living equipped with my right mind.

An attitude of gratitude can operate as the key to open many doors. When we were children, most of our parents taught us to be polite, to say please and thank you. The word thank you is electric. Thank the person who gave you this book. Thank the person who opened the door for you at the supermarket. Thank the person who watched your kids while you were at work or going shopping. Thank the person who gave you information you needed. Thank you holds no pressure of emotion but raises your vibration 100-fold. Just say thank you to people who do you good. As, again, we are all connected, it does as much for them as it does for you.

Practicing gratitude can free you from stress, relieve anxiety, and help you get through and to the next moments of your life. It can bring you to a place of enlightenment, that easy feeling where life still happens but when it does, we have an increased spiritual and intellectual insight and awareness that gives us ease. You cannot force it. Pure gratitude is not flattery. It needs to be honest and real. In exchange, it will provide you with a knowing that despite all that is happening around you, you are at peace, and it is well with your soul.

If you get quiet, you will find truth, happiness, and peace in a place you never dared look. Inside of yourself. Having an attitude of gratitude is more than a cute cliché. It is not snake oil. It is not a magic potion or a cure-all. In the midst of tragedy and trauma, finding a spirit of gratefulness is crazy. It is a radical and monumental paradigm shift. However, when you practice finding the good stuff, what is happening around you will have less power over you. Remember to expose the anger, the fear, the darkness. Be honest about it. Shed light on it. Do what you have to do to recover. Then, simply be grateful that you did.

Ready Roll

There is almost no such thing as ready. There is only now. – Hugh Laurie

Imagine you are at the starting line of an Olympic race. You have spent years training for it. It has cost you time, money and sweat equity. You have had to conquer yourself and others just to get in this race. You have been selected out of thousands of contenders to go for the gold.

The referee holds up his gun, aimed at the sky. "On your mark!" He yells at the top of his voice. You position yourself at just the right place on the starting block. "Get set!" You crouch down, preparing for takeoff, your heart thumping wildly against your chest. This is it. This is the moment you have been waiting for, the chance to prove what you're made of. "Go!" You sprint forward, hurling yourself through space, so excited you fall flat on your face in front of thousands seated in the crowd looking, laughing, taunting.

That is how life is sometimes. You make plans, write down your goals and dreams, get excited about them, post them everywhere so you can see them in order to live them. You have a vision for your life, your marriage, your family. You know your purpose and destiny and you prepare for it. Then something comes and hits you upside your head like a ton of bricks. You didn't expect it. It caught you completely by surprise. You never thought something like that could happen to you. A loved one dies suddenly. You or your child contracts a rare, incurable disease. You lose all your money in a bad investment. Your job closes without notice, or you're fired. All of these things bring your forward movement, all your well-laid plans, to a screeching halt. All your readiness did not prepare you for the element of life's surprises.

When I walked down the aisle to get married, when I agreed to live with my husband in sickness and in health, when I envisioned us on the front porch holding hands while sitting joyfully in our rocking chairs, I did not know our happily ever after would turn into a disaster. My husband's controlling behavior began on our honeymoon. I had started my race and fallen on my face.

The thing is, I couldn't let the world know I was a failure. I was ashamed to let the world see. My children could not know. They were happy. They had a dad who took up for them, protected them, played rock-em-sock-em robots with them. Who was I to be sad, miserable, or discontent? Besides, he was not controlling all the time. It was just me in my feelings, being controlled by my emotions. Right?

In 1992, Olympic runner Derek Redmond of Great Britain, was running the 400 meter race. It was the last qualifier. Four years earlier, he had been knocked off the Olympic team for Great Britain in Seoul because of an injury. He took those four years to heal and train heavily. He had won all of his other races prior to this last one, sprinting through the finish line with ease. He was confident he would make the team. He got off to a great start, holding his own. Then suddenly he heard a pop and was thrust into excruciating pain that felled him on the track. He knew he was in trouble. In utter despair, he watched as the rest of the runners passed him by. But he had come to race. He wasn't going to let four years of arduous work go down the tubes. He was determined to finish. He got up and started hopping. Cameras were getting in his face, recording him. Coaches were coming to get him off the field. Then something wonderful happened. His father, Jim, the man who had supported him through his trials, came running onto the field to help his son get to the finish line. Leaning on him Derek limped forward, his face contorted in pain. When Derek covered his face with his hands, his father removed them. There was no shame in falling. There was no shame in getting back up again and, even though hurt physically and in spirit, continuing the race.

There is an ancient proverb that says, "finishing is better than starting" (Ecclesiastes 7:8a NLV). Jesus himself said, as he took his last breath, "It is finished." We have to know when it is over and when we are to get back on the road and finish our race. It may be painful. It may be difficult. Your heart will hurt, and you may have physical bruises or scars. You must know when there is a time for holding on, and a time for letting go so you can finish your race. The race you are responsible for. The thing that you have come into this world to do.

Every abusive relationship does not end in divorce. Sometimes, the person makes a mistake and can be helped when the problem is addressed. When abuse becomes a pattern, however, there are other options you will need to consider. In order to do that, you must understand when the time is for holding fast and when to let go. Whatever you do, don't forfeit your race.

When life beats up on you, choose to finish. Be determined to finish. No matter that you fell prostrate on the ground in front of the crowd. Finish. No matter that people laughed, jeered, and called you a loser. Don't allow them to usher you off the field. No matter that they said you will never and you cannot. Finish. Finishing is a fight. Falling does not mean you failed. Gather your strength, get up, and start again.

There were times when we were living in hotels infested with bed bugs and roaches. Times when we lived fancy for a night. Times when I did not know where we would lay our head next. I wanted to turn back. I wanted to quit. It was crazy difficult. But my bonus father, Willie Lee Daniels, told me, "you can do this." He held me in his arms and whispered in my ear, "you will be alright." His words, his encouragement helped me gather my strength and start again.

What matters is your decision to fail forward. What matters is your determination through tears, anger, frustration, fear, loss, and grief to keep going. Accept that there will be challenges, judgements, stigmas, and prejudices. Getting to the finish line is not easy. Be patient and compassionate with yourself.

Derek did not win his mete, but when he got up, when he failed forward, the crowd cheered. When his dad came to assist him, the avalanche of sound, the outpouring of love moved them forward. Derek may not have won his race, but he made people see that the Olympics are about more than winning medals. It is the stage where champions compete. Where falling forward despite difficulty can also be a win. That the true spirit of ettin

If you stare too long at a future you cannot predict, you will get depressed and discouraged by the unknown. Focus on the present. That is the gift. There is a new starting line. Position yourself. Take that first step off the block again. You will find energy in the moment that you need it. When you make one move you will connect with the next step. You will learn and know one thing you can do even if that next thing is putting your feet on the floor and standing up.

Derek Redmond had a team of people to assist him and help him recover. You too will need a support team. You will have to surrender your independence for interdependence. Your team will have to be a group of high caliber individuals you can trust with your life. Whether you stay or leave, this is not a race you can do alone. This new challenge will be long term. You and they will need stand-ability, endurance, and commitment. If you choose to leave an abusive relationship, you will have to find people who are trustworthy. You will have to be extremely strategic and your plan tight.

Unlike Derek's 400 meter sprint, leaving an abusive relationship is not a sprint. It is a decathlon and there is really no training for it. I made an agreement with myself to fight because winning, whatever that looked like, was going to be worth it. The gold medal was my peace of mind and a better future for my children. That's what kept me going. Derek had to build up physical muscle and emotional stamina. You will have to do the same. Get yourself ready. Get yourself physically ready. I moved things to storage secretly. Get yourself spiritually ready. Christians call it getting prayed up. If you don't pray, meditate, take walks, get quiet, listen to your spirit's guidance. Get your team together. I worked with counselors, a domestic abuse agency, and lawyers. I had a few friends, an extremely small circle, that I could trust to help me cover my tracks, keeping myself, my family, and friends out of harm's way.

My bonus dad used to talk about sleeping "ready roll." He explained to me that ready roll was when you slept in your clothes and got out of the bed ready to go. When life hits you with an abrupt sharp turn, you will have to find ways to arise ready to roll. To live in the moment while you progressively move forward. Every night when you fall asleep is the end of the journey for that day. You cannot change what you did or did not accomplish. Your day is now the past. Every morning you are born anew, born again into a world unknown. When you are blessed to awake, "clothed and in your right mind" as the old folks used to say in church, it is to a new opportunity, a new sunrise, a new challenge, idea, or inspiration. You have been given another chance to choose again. The starting line has moved. That very thing that you thought would hold you back may be the thing that propels you into your destiny and a glorious future yet unseen.

If you are determined to finish your race as I am, make a commitment to yourself to sleep every night ready to roll the next day. Make a list of the things you need to do. Plan. Prepare. Whatever challenge you are currently facing, ask yourself what response will move your forward in the face of it. Who will you need on your team to help you? Do you know them by name and if not, where can you find them? List them. Contact them. Do whatever you can, whatever you need to move you and your family forward. Every time you wake up, the timer starts. Do whatever you can in the moments you are alive. Prepare yourself to live life on your terms. Get yourself ready so you can be set to GO!

The Next Level

Sometimes when you risk everything, you lose everything too...or so it seems at the time.- Bruce Wilkinson

Everything is built on precepts. One building block at a time, we come to our own levels of understanding in our own time frames. The next level, a phrase often used when referring to relationships, is different for every individual. People in intimate relationships often associate the next level with sex, commitment, marriage, buying a house, living together, or having children. For a lot of us though, taking it to the next level means leaving it behind, leaving it alone, or just leaving!

I had to decide what taking it to the next level meant for me in my relationships. As my children got older, the next level meant letting go so they could grow, fly, or fall. It meant not coming to their rescue so much, allowing them to make their own mistakes, deal with their own consequences. It meant giving them more responsibility and encouraging accountability so they could live independently of me.

The next level in my marriage was learning to love myself enough to protect myself, my children, and our spirits. That eventually entailed leaving my sheltered and secure life to walk out into thin air. It meant facing my fear of the unknown and the unpredictable, putting my hands to the plow and moving forward without looking back.

The next level in my friendships and associations has meant constant change. I had to disassociate from people who spat negative all over my dreams and those who secretly sabotaged me. I had to love some family and friends from a distance for both my safety and my sanity. I am continuously meeting new people who become family not related by bloodline, the extended or bonus family that gives me connection, mentorship, and support.

Life is capricious, ever changing. In all phases and stages of life, we human beings need someone to share our experiences with. Alone we die. We need someone to grow with or to grow us up. We need to shake someone or be shaken ourselves. We need to speak life or have life spoken to us. We need each other. We need change instigators and motivators, transformers to help us get to that next level.

The next level is always about change. Change is a mandate we cannot refuse. We may curse, cry, flail our arms, and try to make things go back the way they once were. We scream. We pray. We say it's not fair. We blame, justify, and repent. At some point, usually when all else has failed, we relent, accepting what is. When we refuse to change or to grow, we end up lost or stuck. We are, however, naturally encoded with adaptability. Even painful things like separation, divorce, and death take us to the next level.

I shared earlier that my daughter really didn't know who I was until I left my abusive marriage. Before then, all she saw in me was mom and Mr. Peter's wife. That's it. It wasn't until after I left that she saw me as courageous, determined, and strong. She saw me beyond the titles and vocations. Someone once told me, if you want to see who a person really is, pray for pressure. Pressure will reveal who a person is at their core. Pressure will show you yourself.

Life happens. Storms come with howling mercenary winds tearing up everything in their paths and scaring us to death. Flood tides rise high enough for us to drown in, sweeping away everything we love, know, and depend on. The fires of life singe us to the very core leaving us scarred, bruised, and barely breathing. Life can be tough. We cannot decide when, where, or how the storms will come or how severe they are going to be. We do not get to control them or plan them out. Rain, snow, sleet, hail, fog, drought – none of these things discriminate. It falls on all of us at the most inconvenient times. Settle that. You partner is not possessed though he or she may be under the influence. It is not a sin to have bad days, moments, or even to make bad decisions. It is life and when life deals you a bum hand, decide how you are going to play it. Grieve, cry, wallow for a time if you must. Take time to feel your sorrow. You will, eventually, have to decide whether to play the hand you are dealt, ask for a new one, or fold. Not deciding is a decision in itself.

I have indeed felt great loss. I lost my home. I lost connection with people I loved. I lost my livelihood. It seemed, at the time, that I had lost everything that was dear to me. But I did not lose my mind. I gained my peace. I traded up. I asked for a better hand. I got a better life in return. It wasn't easy at first. I struggled. It was terrifying, dangerous, and difficult. But my children have great memories of a new world that they would have never seen or experienced if I had not made the decision to change their environment. They would have never experienced daily walks on the beach and playing around in the ocean. They would not have known what it was like to feed the ducks and turtles on science day and visit the zoo on Sundays. They would not have experienced hide-n-seek after dark in our quiet neighborhood or long walks on country roads. They would not have seen dolphins dance in the morning sun or experienced rainbows across the ocean after a storm.

I have never regretted my decision to leave my husband, despite how painful that decision was. Sometimes, "love 'em and leave 'em" is a kindness we give to ourselves and those we love.

7 *CHAPTER SEVEN*

<u>Light Work</u>

You have to find what sparks a light in you so that you in your own way can illuminate the world. — Oprah Winfrey

You are the light of the world. - Matthew 5:14 (KJV)

There is a hymn written by Chris Rice called *Go Light Your World*. My teenage children heard that song when on a mission's trip to Trinidad. The song admonishes us to be a light and take our light to run to and through the darkness, to light up the world.

I have read that we are all light and we come to this planet to give one another light. I have read that "light workers" leave our source with armfuls of that heavenly glow for the express purpose of bringing light to the world. They not only carry light, but they are also themselves light. To be a worker of light, you have to become adept at walking through the darkness without allowing its bleakness and terror to destroy your soul and blow out the candle that is you.

Domestic abuse exists in the darkness of isolation and intimidation. It is a darkness that can demoralize its victims, extinguishing their light. Living in the dark is terrifying to me. It is the darkness that will defy and/or define you. Darkness can be a place of both growth and death.

Most places in Alaska are plunged into darkness for 70 to 80 straight days every year. This darkness can bring about depression, lethargy, and suicidal thoughts. We were born to be light. That does not mean being light will be easy. For a lamp to function, it must be connected to an electrical source. A candle needs fire to ignite it. Fire needs a match, gasoline, and wood to burn. We were born as light. Sometimes, however, we come unplugged. The wick burns low. The wind blows out our flame. What do we do then? What happens when we are faced with the terror of the dark?

Neurologically our brains, flooded with cortisol and adrenalin, change the chemical makeup of our body when we are afraid. This sudden rush of adrenalin causes us to make poor decisions in the moment because of the perceived danger. Our body prepares itself to run, fight, or freeze. When we do not learn how to manage our emotions and that old fight or flight response, our body holds all of our stressors which can, after a time, implode our physical and mental health.

Learning how to deal with stress and conflict that is intertwined in the life of a person being abused is extremely difficult at best. Some things you can do for your physical and psychological well-being are:

- Exercise: Go for a walk around the block a couple of times or even around your back yard mumbling affirmations to yourself. Get yourself grounded by going outside and taking deep breaths in through the nose and out through the mouth. Get a yoga mat and do some floor stretches with your kids. Try yoga or Pilates. Exercise not only boosts your energy, but also increases strength and flexibility. Breathing techniques help us to calm our bodies when we are in fight or flight mode. Movement creates change.
- Don't be afraid or overly concerned about crying. Do not swallow

your tears. Let them go. Crying relieves stress and releases chemicals in your neurosystem that promote healing. It's okay to cry it out.

- Be real with yourself. Resilience, the ability to adapt to adversity, is cultivated. It does not come naturally to us. The best way to cultivate it is to be honest about feelings of anger, rage, loneliness, betrayal, and grief. No one is an island. You don't have to do this by yourself. Get help. Get support.

- Set small goals to build your confidence and share them with your support team so they can keep you accountable. Consider what you did before that helped you get through something difficult. Break it down into small pieces and do it again. Looking at past experiences will also help you to know if you need to change your strategy. This is where writing in a journal can be helpful.

- Project yourself into a future that is free from violence. Take a few minutes or even seconds every day to see that in your mind's eye. Anticipate change.

- Take care of yourself and your needs. Set boundaries where you can. Try to get sleep and rest. The two are not the same. Rest and rejuvenation happens in REM (Rapid Eye Movement) sleep, the place where you are dreaming or relaxed. When you sleep, your brain cleans up all the stuff of the day. Take that fifteen minute break at work, go to the car, and rest your eyes and your mind. Listen to a short meditation. You will be surprised at how rejuvenated you feel once you allow your mind a bit of rest.

- Whenever possible, do something that brings you joy. Ride a bike, paint, sing, play an instrument, play with your children, read a book, or listen to music.

- Don't ignore problems. Ignoring problems will cause stress to build up in your mind and body. Too much stress built up over time can negatively affect your physical and mental health. Talk to a mental health professional you feel comfortable with if you feel you are not making progress.

Lightwork is heavy lifting, and you must equip yourself to do it. Light needs a source and a resource. It is paramount, as in all light, to connect with the source for reignition. Whether that source is scientific information, Spirit, God, Allah, Mother Nature, whatever or whomever you want to call what ignites you, it is imperative that you connect. You may have to be like David and encourage yourself. You may have to be like Moses and seek out a burning bush - someone, or something to give you courage and strength. I listened to a lot of *Goalcast* videos, uplifting music, and meditation on healing and recovery.

To recover your light, you will have to guard your ear gate, what you listen to. Negativity may come for your five senses. You will have to guard your eye gates, what you are exposing yourself to on tv, internet and social media. It has been found that too much continued exposure to social media can cause depression. You begin to see your life through the pictured storied lives of others and feel you don't measure up. Limit time spent watching the news and scrolling on social media.

Be conscious of what you are saying over yourself and what other people are speaking over and about you. Affirm yourself. When you hear yourself, even in your mind, speaking negative about yourself, capture the thought. Speak to it. Say no, not true, that is a lie. Capture and negate that thought and you will recover your right mind.

This may all sound like mumbo jumbo, but they are the things that kept me from losing my mind and losing myself when I was in some very dark places. Keeping your candle lit, keeping your light burning is work. Have you ever seen someone light a fire with sticks? As a girl scout, I was never able to accomplish this feat. Lighters also scared me because I was not able to correctly manipulate them and was afraid of burning myself. I was more adept at starting a fire with matches. Find what keeps your light alive. Grab the tools in your arsenal that you need to preserve your fire.

Some places you can walk through with a candle glow. Other places you will need a torch. Still others, you cannot carry fire, you have to become fire. Figuratively, you will need to be an arsonist, burning down everything in your mind and heart that would destroy you.

Keeping my flame alive meant I had to dig deep into the subconscious to find out what I believed about myself, my health, money, relationships. I did a great deal of reading and self-examination. I operated on myself, tearing down, piece by piece, the things that kept me tied to my past, bound by lies and deception, and delivery from what had become negative core beliefs. I had to burn down the foundation that had been built by and for me and rebuild a new edifice to stand on.

Jesus said he was the light of the world. His light was not extinguished by death but burned brighter. Thousands more people followed "the way" after his death than had followed him in life. This proves to me that when we let our light shine, when we refuse to be extinguished by our circumstances, we illuminate the path for others to follow. When we become fire, we burn down the edifice of deceits and detours that derail us from living our best life and reaching our destinies. Not just for ourselves but as a beacon for others that are obscurely watching us.

Equip yourself to be light. Be a candle. Be a torch. Be fire. Enlighten yourself and change your house, your neighborhood, your community, your world.

Remember to Forget

She remembered who she was and the game changed. – Lalah Delia

Forgetting those things which are behind, and reaching forth for those things which are before… – Philippians 3:13b (KJV)

My second dad, Pop Willie, died from complications due to Alzheimer's. Alzheimer's is a thief. It is a disease that affects memory, cognitive thinking, and behavior. Pop Willie could remember things from decades ago in detail. I loved listening to the animated stories he told about his childhood, growing up in a sharecropping family in Valdosta, Georgia's deep south. Stories about life during the depression, the civil rights movement, World War II, and Vietnam.

Pop Willie never graduated high school. In fact, like many other southern children of his day, he dropped out of school in the fifth grade to go to work. He was still one of the smartest, sharpest, creative, hardworking, educated men I knew. He taught me things that textbooks couldn't. Things American schoolbooks did not dare write about. His favorite story though, was one in which he walked several miles down dirt roads to go in town to see the "picture show."

In Pop's day, you could watch the picture show (the movies) all day for the price of one thin dime. One day, Pop stayed too late and had to walk through miles of dirt roads and corn fields in the dark to get back home. Mind you, this was during a time when the white supremacist hate group known as the Klu Klux Klan was flourishing in the south, killing Black men, women, and children. Pop was barely a teenager. He got a ride a little way but had to walk the rest. He wasn't scared of the Klan. He was scared of his momma. She had told him to be home by a certain time and he was extremely late.

Standing six feet two, with sharply chiseled features, a short, neat afro and boyish grin, his hazel eyes shining, my handsome stepfather would tell us the story of how he tried to outwit his momma. Something he had thought out all the way home on that dark walk. His beautiful dark skin glowed, and his brilliant smile showed off the crinkles on the side of his eyes while he stood in the kitchen, always the kitchen, dramatizing the tale of how he tried to avoid getting a "whoopin" by intending to chop off his big toe. He had decided he would use the ax they used for chopping wood in the back of the house. His silent laughter would bend him sideways as he demonstrated how he was "fitnah" chop off his big toe with that ax after he had come home well after midnight. How his younger brother squealed on him before he could follow through. Pop would throw back his head, mimicking his brother hollering, "Mommmaaaa! Willie Lee fitnah chop off his big toe. Mommmaaa!" We would all laugh as he laughed.

He would tell that story repeatedly. My children and I would never tire of hearing it. Mostly because of how he told it in his deep southern accent and over the top dramatizations.

As his disease progressed, the man I looked up to and loved so much, could still remember that story and many others from his past, but he had forgotten my name. After a while, he also forgot my face calling me a stranger, a white woman, my complexion so light. Alzheimer's robbed me of my hero, whose arms had held me in silent fatherly companionship as we watched TV together. Who, when I left my abusive husband, reassured me with "It's alright? You gonna be alright." I believed him. The man whose arms I had run into when my grandfather, Pop-Pop, died. The man who, with my mom, came all the way to Virginia to surprise me with a new car because he said I would need one in the south. Because of Alzheimer's, because I did not exist in his childhood memories, it was as if I never existed in his life at all.

Our memories work in three stages: encoding, storage, and retrieval. It is an elaborate neuro filing system. We retain sensory memory for milliseconds, short term memory for about 30 seconds, and long-term memories indefinitely. These long-term memories include anything we have played repeatedly in our minds. The more things are repeated, the longer the memory is retained. Every life experience, especially those we have rehearsed in our mind, influences how we do life and what we believe about our lives. Pop Willie and his picture show story were encoded in his long term memory.

We all have memory data that can be triggered by a scent, a song, a similar event, place, or time. It would be wonderful if only the good things were retained. Our retention and encoding, however, is not that selective. Our sensory memory only last for milliseconds in order to spare us all the information that comes at us on a daily basis. If we retained all of that we would be overwhelmed and anxious. With our short-term memory, we retain what is important to us, yet it too can only store a minimal amount of information for a few seconds and, on rare occasions, an entire minute. However, the more an action, a feeling, a thought, a story is repeated, the more likely it is to download into our long-term memory and retained indefinitely. We draw on this long-term memory to function. Whenever we give memory meaning, we retain it longer and closer to the surface. The children's movie, *Inside Out*, explains imagination, emotion, feelings, and memory best.

Abuse, childhood neglect, the shame and guilt occurring after a rape, the rape itself, when rehearsed, can stay locked in our memories indefinitely, triggered by what seems inconsequential. If the abuse happened as an infant or small child, the encoding becomes part of that child's makeup, impacting the child's behavior. Memories become core to why, what, and how we think and believe about ourselves, our community, and the world. Troubling memories of abuse, neglect, threats, shame, and guilt can rear their ugly heads like the seven serpents of Medusa. Spewing the venom of our past, sinking their scary angled fangs into our thoughts, they poison our spirit, our reason, and our actions. For this reason, psychological and emotional abuse can leave deep often undetectable mental scarring.

Time does not heal all wounds. More than two decades after my husband and I separated, I continued struggling with the effects of gaslighting and psychological manipulation. I second guessed myself, struggled with depression, anxiety, guilt, social withdrawal, and isolation. I had nightmares and flashbacks. I once walked into a house to do a clean-out. The layout was exactly like the house I had lived in with my ex where the abuse had reached its critical point. I had a panic attack. It had been seven years since the divorce, 18 years since my leaving. Walking through that house, memories came flooding back. I ran out and could not begin, much less finish, the job. I didn't know then I was suffering from PTSD.

Verbal assault, dominance, control, isolation, ridicule, the use of intimate knowledge-those secrets you share only with your partner-are used to degrade you. Symbolic violence instigated by a look, a hand signal, a nod as a warning are all powerful weapons in the arsenal of an abuser. Their effects can be encoded in its victims for life.

What do you do with all this memory overload? How do you unravel and delete all of the encoding? You have to remember to forget. Forgetting is not ditching the memory. That is impossible. Forgetting is about dealing with the thing that hurt you, so it no longer has control over you. The more you deal with it, the less you will rehearse it in your mind. The less you rehearse it, the more it loses its power. This is not about erasing what happened. The brain does not work like that. What happened to you was real and filed into your mental system. You cannot pull it out. You can, however, take away its power.

I tell my children, never go through anything without getting something good out of it. Search for that thing like hidden treasure, as if your life depended on it, because it does. You may never forget what happened to you. It will never leave the subconscious mind once planted. You will have to put something more powerful over it in order for that thing not to control your life. You have to pry the steering wheel from the grip of your nightmares by addressing them and remembering to forget.

Do not forget to remember. Remember who you were before you were a spouse, partner, girlfriend, significant other. Remember who you were before all the labels were attached to you, the negative programming spoken over you. Dig deep. Not just for what makes you sad. What makes you happy? What things give you joy? Write them down. What things make you feel at peace, at home with yourself? Journal, create art, get therapy, play sports, write some affirmations. Speak aloud where you want to be, not where you are. Read or listen to books like "What to Say When You Talk to Yourself" by Shad Helmstetter; All the Joy You Can Stand by Debrena Jackson Gandy; Divorce: God's Will? By Stephen Gola; How to Unfuck Yourself by Gary John Bishop; and The Verbally Abusive Relationship by Patricia Evans. [See book list in Resources at the end of this book.] Read for 30 minutes or 15 pages a day. Write affirmations and read those to yourself with meals three times a day like medicine. Create new, positive, happy memories with family and friends. If your family is abusive, create a family of friends and others who care about you. Family is not necessarily a bloodline.

Seven years ago I lost my firstborn son. For six years, all I could see when I thought of him was the day he died. His hand trying to sqeeze mine in his while I wept. The beeping of the monitors that alerted me that he was passing. His last breath. My hand pressing on the heart that had stopped beating, incredulous that I could no longer feel it. Hysterically fighting not to leave him. Returning to the smell of the white plastic body bag they had not yet zipped closed over his pale white face. October 17, 2014 he was gone. I could not recall anything more of his life until the end of March 2021. I had a vivid memory of him at about five years old. His chubby chipmunk cheeks and happy smile telling me he was going to be a "rocket star" when he grew up. The memory was so wonderful I decided to call him to share. Then it was there again. Like an ice cold shower or a hard slap in the face. He was gone.

Days later I realized that I was just beginning to remember to forget. The good memories were coming back because, in the long run, I had known him alive more than I had known him dying. The memories of his death still come, but increasingly they are overshadowed by the memories of his life and all we were blessed to share. The goodness of him. His courage, strength, and enduring love. How his life saved other lives. How in the 29 short years he was here, he made a difference in the lives of strangers he would never know or see.

Remember you are more than your circumstances. You are more than what happened to you. You are more than your body, your intelligence, or beauty. More than your limitations, failures, and successes. Of the millions of sperm rushing through the womb to penetrate an egg, you were the strongest, the fastest, and the best no matter the circumstances of your birth. From the beginning, you chose you. Continue to choose you and remember to forget those things which are behind, straining forward with all your might to reach the things you dream of becoming, doing, and seeing.

<u>Hold On to Happy</u>

For every minute you are angry, you lose sixty seconds of happiness. — *Ralph Waldo Emerson*

Love is that condition in which the happiness of another person is essential to your own. — *Robert A Heinlein*

I love to dance. It was forbidden in our house when I was a kid. My mom was a devout Christian woman. She meant well. I am thankful for the spiritual foundations she laid for us all. Unfortunately, however, dancing was forbidden in the Pentecostal doctrine so that, and 'secular' music was not allowed in our house. This did not stop me from doing leaps and pirouettes throughout the house, pretending to tap dance in my patent leather shoes with the thick soled heels, and swaying and bopping to the music my older brothers hid and played in their room or on my mom's stereo when she wasn't home.

As teenagers, my brothers were DJ's. I used to envy them going to the forbidden dances every weekend. Even when mom would lock them out of the house for missing curfew, she couldn't stop them from playing music.

For years I would hide my dancing. I would go in the basement and teach myself ballet, modern, African interpretive, and contemporary dances I had seen on television. Mom only let us watch PBS which meant I was privy to some excellent programming. I saw Mikael Baryshnikov fly and suspended in the air for the first time. Watching him, I believed I could fly too. I didn't mind the bumps and bruises I got trying.

Dance is the celebration of the soul. It says life is good and I am glad I am in it. You can see that when you watch children dancing. They jump, leap, run, fall down, shake, and enjoy themselves all the time without caring whether or not someone is looking or judging them. Their little bodies live out the joy and exuberance that is inside of them, no music necessary. Running, skipping, leaping, tumbling, even falling is no big deal to them. They just get back up and run again. They know how to find joy in the simple things. A worn out box becomes a doll house, a race car, a secret hideout. Crumpled paper becomes an airplane or a mini basketball. Children know how to find joy. They put up a fuss when mom says it's time to leave the playground, put the game away, or leave the rubber duck in the tub. They are trying to hold on to happy. Who wants to let go of their happy place? Who wants to let go of joy, laughter, and fun, to do homework, eat dinner, go to bed, get dressed or visit someone or somewhere that requires them to sit quietly with their hands folded in their laps? Children hold on to happy for dear life.

At the time I started drafting this book, my youngest was seven years old. I swear Ryan (not his real name) only closed his eyes to recharge his batteries. REM sleep eluded him. The first thing he did every morning was ask questions. I swore he thought them up in his sleep. Once he woke up at twelve midnight and yelled from his room, startling me awake.

"Mommmmyyy!"

"Yes Ryan. What's wrong?"

"Do lions lay eggs?"

We had a fifteen minute discourse on the birthing habits of lions, chickens, and humans before he could fall back to sleep. I, of course, was wide awake.

The constant questions were just the revving of Ryan's engines. He absolutely had to show me his newest back, front, side flip techniques. I was an audience of one as he practiced his Michael Jackson moves for the school talent show. He was actually an extremely talented dancer. He pulled my arm to witness his running speed, football prowess, read the newest story he had written, or his latest something. He was a bundle of activity and could be exhausting to keep up with. He was open, honest, funny, frank, and absolute genius at seven.

Add four other equally precocious and extremely active children to the mix and you had my household. Multiply that by the constant flow of their friends running in and out of the house. Watch them harness and harmonize all that energy and you will understand what it meant to be joy-full.

Children find joy in the trivial things. A melody they make up in their heads and sing repetitively. Jumping rope. I watched my daughter who did not make the cheerleading squad, rehearse cheers she had learned at practice, teaching them to all the neighborhood kids. It didn't matter to her that she didn't make the squad. She enjoyed the experience.

If you want to learn how to be filled with joy, look at little children. If your children are not joyful, happy human beings, look at your environment and look at you.

I taught my sons how to climb trees by climbing trees myself, something I had always enjoyed doing as a child and continued to the age of fifty. I loved sitting up high in the branches, resting on the gnarly limbs. I used to play in the rain with my children. Take them out in their bare feet and run with them down the sidewalk splashing in the puddles, something their father would not have appreciated had he been home. I taught my children to appreciate the turning of the leaves and the glory of nature. I sat them down to watch sunsets, made up silly stories for them, and wrestled with them all at one time.

No matter our misery, I always found ways to give them a reason to smile, laugh and have fun. What is life without joy? I did not want them to remember only grief and struggle. I did not want their young spirits to be broken by the trauma we had experienced.

When was the last time you walked in the rain, tasting rain drops on your tongue? When was the last time you laughed from your belly and smiled till your face hurt? When was the last time you danced for no reason, made funny faces at yourself in the mirror, clowned around, read a book you enjoyed? When was the last time you decided to put misery away for a moment and be happy?

I once heard happiness defined as temporary insanity. It is all right to go a little crazy to get to your happy place. When you get to it, hold on for as long as you can. It will be a memory that sustains you in the tough times. Hold on to happy like your life depended on it because it does.

Practice Peace

Knowledge is of no value unless you put it into practice. — Anton Chekhov

Throughout this journal I have advocated for meditation, yoga, journaling, gratitude, choosing, affirmations, and letting go. No matter how many times you read these things, think about them, even meditate on them, none of it works for the long haul unless you make it a practice. Ask any bodybuilder or anyone on a weight loss challenge. Muscles do not form overnight. Unless you lift the weights and put down the chocolate chip cookies on a regular basis you will not see the results you want. The mind is a muscle and if we are to change our mind, we have to challenge it.

We have been programmed with so much negativity that we automatically react rather than respond to situations and circumstances. Changing our navigation system is a difficult process. Reprogramming takes time and learning a new way of doing things take practice. Like a GPS, we often have to recalculate.

The first time I tried to meditate, I couldn't shut my mind down for two whole seconds. I could not find my 'happy place.' I learned, with further practice and research, different ways of meditating. I was exhilarated when I found dance meditation. It is a fun, enjoyable, and naturally creative way that helped me release emotions through body movement. My favorite is a fifteen minute guided meditation with Sheer Lev called *Guided Dance Meditation for Emotional Release*. There are several other ways to meditate as well. If you are a spiritual person, then pick your favorite scripture, proverb, or saying then sit quietly and meditate on that for a few minutes a day to gain clarity and focus. Another thing that works for me is sitting beside the ocean or walking in nature. You can find your own unique ways. (See some resources at the end of this book.)

Meditation is not spooky, new, or even new age. It has been in practice for over 5,000 years. King David meditated. He wrote in Psalms 1:2,3 that those who meditated would be like trees planted by rivers of water bearing fruit in their season. I have observed trees planted near the river's edge. Their roots are deep and firm. In storms they tend to bend rather than break. They have become flexible even though they are dense wood.

Meditate means to ponder, think about, reflect on. David reflected on the scriptures and the truths they held for him. Monks, priests, executives, athletes, and homemakers have all used meditation for its health and healing benefits. When I was in the hospital, a nurse commended me on using meditation. He shared with me that there was a study that found patients, especially those with chronic illnesses, benefitted more from meditation than medicine and were able to recover more quickly. I can attest to that. Getting quiet and connecting with your inner self is not something to be afraid of.

Meditation offers some amazing benefits including:

- Reducing stress thus decreasing and controlling anxiety, depression, chronic pain, and strain on the heart which also helps to decrease high blood pressure.
- Helps to promote emotional health by increasing clarity, focus, creative problem solving, and positivity.
- Proper breathing and relaxation techniques enhance physical health and well-being resulting in better sleep, more self-control, and less physical tension. This can cause a reduced damaging buildup of cortisol from the fight, flight, or freeze response.
- Excessive worry results in damage to the hippocampus which can result in memory loss. Meditation reduces not only age-related but also stress-related memory loss, enhancing attention instead.

If you want to live on purpose, if you want to move along your path, practice the perfect things. Practice loving yourself and being more compassionate towards yourself. Practice speaking more positively by using healthy affirmations so that you can grow your self-confidence. Practice re-designing your life with vision boards and journaling about what you want. Practice developing and elevating yourself by learning new skills, finding a mentor, a coach, a therapist. Practice gratitude for the good things in your life. Practice physical exercise by taking a walk, going to the gym, dancing in the rain. Practice joy by smiling at yourself in the mirror and laugh whenever you get the chance.

When you practice, you can lessen your anxiety, and your love will expand. Your understanding will grow and your mental toughness increase. Do not practice with the ever elusive goal of attaining perfection. You will not always know what the right thing is to do, but you will be more equipped to do what feels right for you at the time. All you can do is the best you can with the information you have at hand.

To be perfect means you recognize that all you can do is all you can do. You can practice the wrong things and make a perfect mess. The best you can do is recognize that you are perfectly imperfect and to find peace with that.

Forgiveness-The Last Word

The weak can never forgive. Forgiveness is an attribute of the strong.– Mahatma Gandhi

Forgiveness is not always easy. At times, it feels more painful than the wound we suffered, to forgive the one that inflicted it. And yet, there is no peace without forgiveness. – Marianne Williamson

There is some good in the worst of us and some evil in the best of us. When we discover this, we are less prone to hate our enemies.– Dr. Martin Luther King Jr.

I could not, in good conscious, write this book without including a chapter on forgiveness. It is hard to know where to begin as I do not have the exact recipe for such a daunting task, nor is there truly one effortless way of doing it. I do believe, however, that the first person we must forgive is ourselves, so let's talk about that

Most often when we speak about forgiveness, we are speaking in reference to forgiving someone who wronged or hurt us in some way. But how can we give to that person what we have not given to ourselves? We carry around the guilt of our faults and faux pas, our lapses in judgement and discretion, and all of our lifelong errors. Our skeletons in the closet whisper to us from their cramped quarters telling us that if people only knew the unspeakable truth about the things we have done, they would not love us or even like us. The skeletons condemn us, and we agree, condemning ourselves. We carry shame for things we did not cause. We carry blame and accusations as if it is our own baggage to claim. We pay a thousand times for our sins. We judge ourselves much more severely than anyone else could, not allotting ourselves the same compassion, kindness, and redemption we give to others.

I know that forgiveness is necessary to move on. They tell me there is no peace without it. There is some truth to that but not always. There are situations where I honestly do not remember ever forgiving the person who wronged me. I just moved on with my life. Maybe that is forgiveness, not allowing another person to have space any more in your mind and heart.

I know, from my experience, that forgiveness is a process. It is not like making instant grits for breakfast. It rarely happens all at once. Forgiveness is a constant work in progress. It is taking baby steps to let go. It is often painful. Fraught with cruel memories and scars still engraved on our bodies, our souls, our hearts, and minds we come to path of forgiveness with trepidation. Staggering upon this path, we must continuously drag ourselves out of the past to stand firmly on the pedestal of our present looking hopefully towards our future. This takes time, sometimes a lifetime.

You and I have both heard, "forgiving is fine as long as you don't forget." I find some truth in that as well. A year after I left Peter, I felt it was safe to bring the children to see him. I brought them every summer, during spring breaks and holidays. He also visited a time or two. I still loved him, still felt connected to him. An abused woman usually leaves her partner an average of seven times before she really leaves him. Peter was still in my heart, so much so that we almost got back together again. It didn't take long however for me to realize that though, on the surface, things were different, that was only the show. In reality, not much had changed. But I had definitely changed. The children had changed and grown. Even Peter had changed, but his philosophy concerning women and marriage had not and, as that was the crux of the problem, there was no reason for me to crucify myself again.

Forgiveness is not forgetting what happened. Your mind has a memory, the tapes rewinding unbidden and in living color. Almost twenty years after I had left, divorced and forgiven Peter, I walked into a house to do a clean-out with a business associate. The layout was exactly the same as the home I had fled. Walking through that house, I started having flashbacks. I hyperventilated. I ran out of the house to breathe and explained to my associate that I wouldn't be able to fulfill my end of the contract and why. That house took me back to the years I lived a nightmare. I went home to recover myself. Forgetting is sometimes not an option. Forgiveness is not synonymous with amnesia.

I knew the hold had been broken and the connecting thread severed when, one day while sitting in my car preparing to leave work, one of my children called me to tell me that Peter had been in a car accident. I asked if he was okay. They said he was fine. Then I told them to take the chicken out of the freezer so I could cook it for dinner. Moments later I realized I didn't feel anything when I learned of Peter's accident. It was as if it had happened to a stranger. Peter no longer had a hold on my mind and heart. I did not hate him, nor did I love him. I wished him no ill, no harm. I cared about my children and how they felt because he was their father but there was nothing beyond that. His hold on me had been broken. I smiled as I started my car.

It is okay to be okay with never going back. It is okay and very normal to still feel the connection after you have left, even if you have gone and returned several times. It is also okay to not feel anything anymore for the person you once loved. Leaving my abusive marriage is a decision I will never regret. I did what was best for all of us, my husband included. Letting go in my heart and mind freed me to move on. Forgiving myself and letting go of the guilt I felt for dragging my children away from all they had known, allowed me to heal which, I am finding, is a constant process.

Martin Luther King's portrayal of forgiveness comes the closest to my perspective. We are all capable of evil. We have all hurt someone by mistake or on purpose, manipulated someone to bend to our will, been selfish, judgmental, and condescending. None of this behavior is loving or kind. Sometimes it happens in a moment. A moment when we are angry. A moment when we are sad. A moment when we are feeling overwhelmed. Knowing this, acknowledging it enabled me to forgive Peter. It did not happen overnight. It took several years until it seemed like suddenly, there were no more open wounds. When the healing was done, I could live again without the baggage that had claimed me.

Women especially are expected, socialized, and pressured to forgive others. We tend to rely on our anger to get us through the pain and that is not necessarily a bad thing. But harboring resentment helps us to justify our negative attitudes and behaviors. It gives us an alibi, an excuse, an out. Blaming ourselves and others is much easier than forgiving. Forgiveness is tremendous work. Forgiving means we have to admit that we are as fallible as the person who mistreated, abused, neglected, or hurt us. It does not mean we lie down and play dead or become carpets for people to step over and crap on. It does not mean we remain deluded and manipulated. It certainly doesn't mean we take the blame for things we did not do, or that we do not hold the other persons accountable for what they did. It is admitting that we are not flawless but are ourselves in need of forgiveness.

Thorough and effective healing must include forgiveness. We must make ourselves a priority in this transaction. We must first forgive ourselves. Accept that we are angry, hurt, and even want revenge. Let's not pretend that there are no evil intentions within us when someone has wronged us. We must face our feelings of guilt, anger, resentment, fear, rage, rejection, jealousy, pain, and even hatred. We have to address and free ourselves of all those things that bind us to our abuser and our past. Allowing bitterness and resentment to fester in our hearts destroys us and those we love.

We cannot begin to forgive anyone unless we first forgive ourselves. That really is the most difficult forgiveness of all. Correct forgiveness of ourselves and others is essential to our recovery. If you would be completely healed, you must submit yourself to the process of forgiveness remembering that the first person you must forgive in order to find peace is you.

8 *Epilogue – The Way Forward*

Quite some time ago, after seeing a news cast of a woman severely beaten by her husband, I asked myself why she didn't just leave this man. I thought he was a monster. I admit I was naïve. I did not understand how complex the partner abuse relationship is. I have since, through my own experience, come to the realization that there is no such thing as "just leave." Leaving is much easier said than done. Often when people ask this question, they are not really interested in the answer. I can't say I really was at the time. I had already judged the woman and her partner. Like most, I wasn't really interested in facts or documentation.

Domestic violence and rape victims are often re-victimized by the court system, religious community, and society at large. Women, especially those in religious communities, are so demonized that almost 80% do not report their abuse. In fear of being ostracized by their local church whose members they call family, in addition to the fear of losing the love of God, most women in religious communities keep silent about their abuse and stay and pray as they are told. In some states, police can press charges against abusers when their spouse or partner will not. This is not the case in every state and still requires the cooperation of the victim to prosecute.

Why is the victim held responsible for the abuser's behavior? Why doesn't anyone ask why the abuser does not just leave? The most dangerous time for battered women, their children, family, and friends is when they leave their abuser. Intimate partner victimization increased by 42% between 2016 and 2018. Rape and sexual assault increased by 146%. At the same time, the risk of femicide-the murder of women-by firearms also increased by a whopping 400% (National Coalition Against Domestic Violence, 2021). These are sobering numbers. But more than numbers, they are human lives. The tally is not in yet for the cost of life during the 2019/2020 pandemic when everyone was sheltering in place.

Writing about domestic violence has been extremely challenging, the weight of it causing me to walk away from it many times, for many years. It was devastating recognizing and understanding the impact of domestic violence on families, communities, and people of all ages, genders, races, socio-economic status, religion, and nationality. But I keep returning to it, mostly because I know that there are people who need to hear this message. My hope is that this book initiates conversation and instigates change. If you are a domestic violence survivor, I hope this book helps you to transition from a place of helplessness to hope. If you are someone trying to navigate through pain, guilt, and shame, I hope this book serves as a roadmap to healing. If you are someone who wants to understand why your friend, co-worker, family member cannot leave his or her abusive relationship, I hope this book is a revelation.

I do not have all the answers. What worked for me may not work for you. You may not agree with some things and cynically question everything. That's okay. Take what you need. Like my mentor used to say, "Eat the fish and leave the bones."

Use this book as a guide to help you find your own answers, your own solutions, your own way. Use the extensive resources listed in the appendix to access more information, educate yourself, get help, or become help for someone in need.

If you are an abuse victim or survivor, I hope this book assists you in recovering yourself and leads you to a safe place without and within.

APPENDIX A – RESOURCE LIST

National Coalition Against Domestic Violence
Provides 24 hour services, assistance, and resources.
https://www.thehotline.org; www.ndvh.org
1-800-799-SAFE (7233)
1-800-787-3224(TTY)
1-855-812-1011(Deaf and Hard of Hearing) (VP)

Office of Women's Health
Helpline: 1-800-994-9662
9am to 6pm (ET) Monday through Friday
www.womenshealth.gov
https://womenshealth.gov/relationships-and-safety/get-help/state-resources

Women Organized Against Rape
www.woar.org
Office: 215-985-3315
24 hour Hotline: 215-985-3333
Philadelphia, PA

Philadelphia Domestic Violence
24 hour Hotline: 1-866-723-3014
215-456-1529 (TTY)

Domestic Violence Services-New Jersey
www.nj.gov
click on Services
click on Division of Youth and Family Services
click on Women
click on Domestic Violence Services

Virginia Sexual and Domestic Violence Action Alliance
https://vsdvalliance.org
24 hour Hotline: 1-800-838-8238
24 hour Text: 804-793-9999
Or chat online
Services, information, resources – Maryland and Virginia

D.C. Alliance Empowering Homicide Survivors Inc.
https://dcaehs.org

"A clearing house for supportive services. Offering a team of trained professionals to assist victims, co-victims, and families of domestic violence and homicide occurring in the Washington, D.C. Metropolitan areas. Helping to rebuild the lives of victims, survivors, and their families."

Advocacy and assistance for domestic violence survivors and families of homicide victims from the initial event until they no longer feel the need for services. Educational training for pastors relating to domestic violence, teen dating violence, and bullying.

Prayer & Support Helpline/Talk Therapy - 240-988-3483

Monday thru Sunday; 7am to 10pm. All calls answered within 24 hours.

Mailing Address: P.O. Box 8753, Hyattsville, MD 20787

Housing/Counseling/Emergency Shelter/ Support

Domestic Abuse Project of Delaware County, Inc.
24 hour hotline: 610-565-4590

https://www.dapdc.org

Open Monday through Friday

8am to 4pm

Email-infor@dapdc.org

Office: 610-565-6272

Media, Pennsylvania

Offers counseling, housing assistance and supports, emergency shelter, advocacy, education.

Domestic Shelters.org
https://domesticshelters.org

National and international domestic violence emergency   shelter information, education, legal resources, and more.

24-hour hotlines available by state and region.

Family Violence Prevention Services
https://fvps.org

24-hour hotline: 210-733-8810

Programs and admin: 210-930-3669 [Texas]
Mission: "To break the cycle of violence and strengthen families by providing necessary tools for self-sufficiency."
Legal assistance, emergency shelter, transitional housing, parenting education, specialized intervention with children, youth, and the elderly.

Women Against Abuse – Safe at Home Program

Domestic Violence 24-hour Hotline: 1-866-723-3014
100 south Broad Street, Suite 1341, Philadelphia, PA 19102
Office Phone: 215-386-1280
Offers relocation assistance, housing supports, counseling, advocacy, education, and more for the Philadelphia region.
https://www.womenagainstabuse.org

Covenant House

https://covenanthouse.org
Provides housing and supportive services for youth facing homelessness and survivors of sex trafficking.
Email: info@covenanthouse.org
Phone: 1-800-388-3888

Services for Teens, Pre-Teens, and Young Adults:

Love is Respect.org

https://www.loveisrespect.org
24-hour Hotline: 1-866-331-9474
24 hour Text: LOVEIS to 22522
Mission: Offers "confidential support for teens, young adults, and their loved ones seeking help, resources, or information related to healthy relationships and dating abuse in the US."
Native American, LGBTQ+, deaf services and more.

Thetrevorproject.org
https://www.thetrevorproject.org
24 hour Hotline: 1-866-488-7386
24 hour Text: text Start to 678-678
Suicide prevention and crisis intervention, information, advocacy, and support for LGBTQ youth.

Becky's Fund
https://www.beckysfund.org
Phone: 202-851-4099
Email: info@beckysfund.org
Emergency support services, resources, and education.
1225 New York Ave, NW/8th floor ; Washington, DC, 20005

1-800runaway.org
24-hour Hotline: 1-800-RUNAWAY (7862929)

Dating Matters® /Funded Programs /Violence Prevention (CDC)
Strategies to promote healthy teen relationships for ages 11-14.
Email: datingmatters@cdc.gov
Phone (24 hours): 1-800-232-4636

Native American and Tribal Women and Girls in Danger

Indian Law Resource Center
Non-profit law and advocacy organization.
https://indianlaw.org/safewomen
406-449-2006
MT@Indianlaw.org
Helena, MT 59601
202-547-2800
Washington, DC
DCOffice@Indianlaw.org

National Domestic Violence Hotline
    1-800-799-SAFE (7233)
    www.ndvh.org

Strong Hearts Helpline
    https://strongheartshelpline.org
    24-hour Hotline: 1-844-7 NATIVE (762-8483)
    "Dating, domestic, and sexual violence helpline for Native
    American and Alaska natives offering culturally appropriate
    support and advocacy."

National Sexual Assault Hotline of the Rape, Abuse, and Incest
    National Network (RAINN)
    1-800-656-HOPE (4673)
    www.rainn.org

National Center for Missing and Exploited Children
    1-800-THE-LOST (1-800-843-5678)
    www.missingkids.com

The National Center for Victims of Crime
    1-800-FYI-CALL (1-800-394-2255)
    1-800-211-7996 (TTY) www.ncvc.org

Educational Toolkits

Domestic Violence Power and Control Wheels
www.thehotline.org
Power and Control Wheel for Immigrant Women
www.futureswithoutviolence.org

In Her Shoes
Educational Toolkit for Teaching About Domestic Violence
Washington State Coalition Against Domestic Violence
http://wscadv.org/resources/in-her-shoes-training-kits/

In Their Shoes
Educational Toolkit about Teen Dating Violence
Washington State Coalition Against Domestic Violence
http://wscadv.org/resources/in-their-shoes

Sharpe Turns
[YouTube Channel]
Videos by K.J. Sharpe featuring *Turning Points* and *Becoming Fire.*

Training for Religious Leaders
Faith Based Domestic Violence Certificate Training
www.focusministries1.org

Clergy Guide on Domestic Abuse
https://www.jwi.org/clergy-guide-on-domestic-abuse
Clergy Task Force to End Domestic Violence in the Jewish Community.

Partnering with Clergy to Prevent Domestic Violence
University of Georgia. https://news.uga.edu/partnering-with-clergy-to-prevent-domestic-violence

APPENDIX B – RECOMMENDED READING LIST

Below is a list of books I read as I was going through my process. There is also a list of interactive meditation videos and other information available on YouTube. Take advantage of these resources to learn more about how to overcome and recover on your journey.

All the Joy You Can Stand - 101 Sacred Power Principles for Making Joy Real in Your Life
Debrena Jackson Gandy
Harmony, ©2000, 2001

Breaking Free From Partner Abuse - Voices of Battered Women Caught in the Cycle of Domestic Violence
Mary Marecek , Morning Glory Press, ©1999

Divorce: God's Will? - The Truth of Divorce and Remarriage in the Bible for Christians
Stephen Gola
Divorce Hope; PO Bo 640, 301 N. Main St., Coudersport, PA 16915
©2003, 2005

The Four Agreements - A Toltec Wisdom Book
A Practical Guide to Personal Freedom
Don Miguel Ruiz with Janet Mills
Amber-Allen Publishing, San Rafael, California, ©1997

In The Meantime – Finding Yourself and the Love You Want
Iyanla Vanzant
Simon and Schuster, ©1998

The Lady, Her Lover, and Her Lord
Bishop T.D. Jakes
Berkley, © 2000

Living with the Ancients – A History of Abuse and Domestic Violence and How it Impacts Women and Girls in Society Today.
K. J. Sharpe, © 2021, 2022. Sharpe Turns Publishing

No Place for Abuse - Biblical and Practical Resources to Counteract Domestic Violence
Catherine Clark Kroeger and Nancy Nason-Clark
InterVarsity Press; Downers Grove, Illinois
©2001

Shattering Our Assumptions - Breaking Free of Expectations, Others and Our Own By
Miriam Neff and Debra Klingsporn
Bethany House Publishers, ©1996

Simple Abundance: A Daybook of Comfort and Joy
By Sarah Ban Breathnach
Grand Central Publishing, ©1995, 2009

Sistah, Can You Feel Me
By K. J. Sharpe
Outskirts Press, ©2010

Surviving Domestic Violence - Voices of Women Who Broke Free
Elaine Weiss, Ed.D, Clinical Professor
Department of Family and Preventive Medicine
University of Utah School of Medicine
© 2000

The Verbally Abusive Relationship - How to Recognize it and How to Respond
Expanded Second Edition
Patricia Evans
Published by Adams Media Corporation, Avon, Massachusetts, ©1992, 1996

Verbal Abuse Survivors Speak Out - On Relationship and Recovery
Patricia Evans
Adams Media Corporation, Avon, Massachusetts
©1993

When Bad Things Happen to Good People
By Harold S. Kushner
Published by Anchor Books, A Division of Random House, Inc., New York, ©1981

When Violence Begins at Home - A Comprehensive Guide to Understanding and Ending Domestic Abuse
By K. J. Wilson
Hunter House, © 1997

[VIDEOS]
Guided Dance Meditation for Emotional Release
Sheer Lev
https://www.youtube.com/watch?v=KRyks99Y9Qc

Learn to Bring Down Stress/Guided Meditation for Kids/Breathing Exercises/Go Noodle
Go Noodle/Get Moving
https://www.youtube.com/watch?v=bRklLioT_NA&t=94s

Sharpe Turns - Fire!
K. J. Sharpe/Sharpe Turns
https://www.youtube.com/watch?v=BNEaUDlBRHE

Sharpe Turns
[Various videos available o YouTube]

APPENDIX C – SAFETY PLANNING

Domestic violence, partner abuse, teen dating violence is described a "the willful intimidation, physical assault, battery, sexual assault, and/or other abusive behavior as part of a systematic pattern of power and control perpetrated by one intimate partner against another. It includes physical violence, sexual violence, threats, economic, and emotional/psychological abuse. The frequency and severity of domestic violence varies dramatically" (National Coalition Against Domestic Violence, 2021).

Following is a list of some abusive behaviors.

- The person believes they are superior and their partner inferior. Believes they have superior intelligence and should therefore make all decisions concerning the couple including who should be their partners friends, where they should go, what they should wear, and more. They are always right.

- Person believes a spouse is to obey without question and when they do not obey, they are to be disciplined.

- Person refuses to acknowledge wrong or take responsibility for actions. When they do or say something wrong, they tell you that you have no sense of humor, can't take a joke, are too sensitive. They blame you for their actions.

- Husband believes that he is the master, head of household, whose word and will is never to be questioned, only followed.

- Person uses children against their partner, continually undermines partner's discipline and familial relationships.

- Partner controls who the person is allowed to see and for how long, where the partner can go and with whom. Closely monitors partner's movements while continually calling the partner untrustworthy.

- Has affairs and blames partner or uses those affairs to control partner and make them feel inferior to keep them in a place of subservience and low self-esteem.

- Partner believes he owns you and thus has rights to do whatever they want with your body no matter how you feel. Has sex with you whenever they choose with no regard for your safety, physical health, or desire. Forces you to participate in sexual activities like orgies, three-some's, sex with strangers, voyeurism. Forces you to have sex against your will.

- Sabotages your job. Doesn't allow you to work. Makes you late for work by hiding keys, taking the battery out of your car, making excuses, starting arguments, causing disruption. Shows up at your job belligerent publicly humiliating and embarrassing you. Calls you frequently at work upsetting you and causing conflict with personal calls at work. Their behavior makes you lose or quit your job.

- Sabotages educational and career advancement including telling you that you are not smart enough or don't need a degree. Tells you to be satisfied with what you have. Crushes your dreams, steals your dreams and profits from them, dismisses and attacks you for dreaming. Tells you that you don't have time and there is no money, that you should just take care of the kids and be happy.

- Empties your bank account. Maxes out your credit cards with no intention of paying the bill. Forces you to pay bills or to constantly give them money.

- Limits your communication. Hides, breaks, or takes phones, pagers, checks laptop or doesn't allow you to have or use one. Monitors all communication devices closely. Listens in on phone calls, checks emails, texts, phone messages, mail, social media even after you break up or separate.

- Threatens to harm your children or take them away from you. Threatens to or actually harms family pets. Threatens to harm themselves if you leave or to harm other members of your family including parents and siblings, or your friends.

- Purposely harms children or pets in an argument with you but says it was a mistake. Takes anger out on children. Causes mental, physical, or sexual harm to children including gaslighting, rape, molestation, battery, and emotional and mental stress through name calling and negative persecution.

- Extremely jealous and controlling nature. Uses jealousy as justification for controlling behavior. Isolates you from family and friends on the basis that they don't love you like he/she does. Tells you they just "want what's best for you" and that they are "trying to protect you" when in reality they are attempting to isolate you from anyone's opinions but theirs.

- Punishes you by withholding attention and affection. Gives you the silent treatment for hours or days. Makes you question what you have done wrong when nothing has happened. Keeps you in a state of worry and fear. Withholds finances, medical treatment including dental work, treatment for bruises, etc., health care for you and your children.

- Uses verbal threats, manipulation, gaslighting, and other forms of psychological manipulation to weaken your resolve and destroy your self-esteem, self-confidence, and self-awareness.

- Threatens you with guns, knives, rape, or any other instrument that can be used as a weapon against you. Tells you that no one will believe you if you tell, especially in the case of marital rape.

- Makes it difficult for you to enter or leave your home. Puts bars on windows and doors, withholds housekeys, insists on moving you and your family far away from relatives and friends.

- Person has violent erratic behavior. They can be calm one minute and fly off the handle the next for no apparent reason, calling your names, criticizing everything you do, terrorizing you in word and deed, insulting you, and dismissing anything you have to say. Creates an atmosphere of fear in the home. Person has a need to be feared. It feeds their low self-esteem and helps them avoid personal accountability.

- Tries to tell you how you feel, what you think, and how things should be done. Tries to take control of your thoughts, including how you feel about yourself and others. Disregards your opinions and teaches your children to be distrustful of you, sabotaging your relationship with them by making you appear stupid or nonsensical.

- Person attempts to normalize abusive behavior by blaming and saying that it happens in all families.

Personal Safety Planning

Leaving an abusive partner is the most empowering thing you can do for yourself, your children, and your loved ones. To leave safely requires strategic planning and support. Prepare to leave permanently as returning to an abuser will increase the risk of further, more dangerous levels of abuse. Ask yourself the following questions:

1. When and how am I going to leave? You know more than anyone what is the safest time for you.
2. Who can help me? Make sure these persons are not affiliated with your partner in any way, even if they are on your side.
3. What support systems will I need to put in place? Start gathering together information and resources. Do not use your home computer. Go to the library and keep information somewhere safe.
4. Who do I trust to keep my plans a secret? Get help from local organizations. If possible, avoid any that your partner may be affiliated with, especially if the person is a police officer, member of the clergy, or other person in authority. Check the national hotline for help.
5. Where am I going, how am I going to get there, and who can help me safely reach my destination?

Remember you are not alone. If you are in crisis and do not know what to do, contact the National Domestic Violence Hotline at 1-800-799-SAFE (7233). Dial 911 if you are in immediate danger. Visit www.ncadv.org; www.thehotline.org for more detailed information on developing a safety plan.

Some things to prepare ahead of time.

1. Pack personal papers ahead of time and keep them in a safe place away from the house where you can easily retrieve them. These include:
   - Birth certificates for yourself and your children

- Driver's license
- Medical records
- Social security cards
- Restraining order with several copies if you have one.
- Passports, green cards, work permits
- Health insurance cards, life insurance, vehicle registration and insurance paperwork.
- Child support, custody, divorce, or legal separation papers.
- Children's school records.
- Medicines for yourself and your children including any prescriptions and over the counter medications.
- Up-to-date pictures of yourself, your children, and your abuser.
- List of shelters and emergency contact numbers.
- Items of sentimental value to you and your children.
- Credit card transactions are traceable. Use cash if possible. You can also transfer funds from a credit account to a prepaid card you can purchase locally.
- Have an extra set of car keys, house keys, keys to safety deposit box etcetera.
- Pack clothing, accessories, and toiletries for yourself and your children in case you have to leave quickly.

2. The following safety precautions are also recommended:
   - Have a safe word for you and your children. Change this word every few days or every two weeks. Make sure teachers, the school principal, employers know this safe word.
   - If you feel you are going to be abused, call 911. Make sure you give the person the address.
   - Stay out of the kitchen and any place where there are possible weapons. Try to be near an exit.

- Teach your children how to dial 911 and what it is used for.
- Have safety drills in the home when your partner is not there. Teach your children how to get out of the house quickly just as you would practice a fire drill.

How Friends, Family, and Clergy Can Help

1. Don't judge, criticize, or condemn. Be attentive, listen. When you see signs of physical battery, don't ignore it. Let the person know you are there for them if they need help. If you see something, get to a safe place and call police.
2. Never blame the victim, underestimate her fears, joke about her situation, or say things like, "If I were you...." Never tell them what they have to do or what a jerk their partner is. This will only cause the person to feel defensive. Offer your help but don't force anything.
3. Be aware that the victim and her children may be in danger. Visit as often as you can. Call. Stay connected. Be involved in her life. Give support. Be a safe space.
4. Call the National Domestic Violence Hotline if you need to talk to someone about your concerns.
5. Clergy must acknowledge that domestic violence exists, even when it comes from among their own leadership and bring the offender into accountability.
6. Clergy must be educated on domestic violence and how to address it.
7. Churches can connect with local authorities, social service agencies, shelters, and domestic violence advocacy organizations to get information and disseminate in and among their congregation.
8. Churches can host an *In Her Shoes* and *In Their Shoes* presentations.
9. Clergy can get training at www.focusministries1.org and www.thehotline.org.
10. Contact your members of congress in the house and senate and ask them to expand the federal definition of domestic violence to include dating violence and stalking. Ask them what they are doing

in support of legislation that provides funding for programs that provide help to children, youth, and adult victims of domestic violence, abuse, sex trafficking, and teen dating violence. Ask them about increasing funding for the Violence Against Women Act (VAWA) programs.

REFERENCES

Abi-Habib, M., & Raj, S. (2019, February 9). Nun's Rape Case Against Bishop Shakes a Catholic Bastion in India. *The New York Times*. https://nytimes.com/2019/02/09/world/asia

Baird, J., & Gleeson, H. (2018, October 22). "Submit to your husbands": Women told to endure domestic violence in the name of God - ABC News (Australian Broadcasting Corporation). https://mobile.abc.net.au/news/2017-07-18/domestic-violence-church-submit-to-husbands/8652028?

Cole, J., Symes, C., Coffin, J., & Stacey, R. (2012). *Western Civilizations, Their History & Their Culture: Combined Volume* (Brief Third Edition). W. W. Norton. (Original work published 2005)

Edwards LMFT, B. G. (2019, February 26). *Alarming Effects of Children's Exposure to Domestic Violence*. https://www.psychologytoday.com/us/blog/progress-notes/201902/alarming-effects-childrens-exposure-domestic-violence

Fromm, E. (2006). *The Art of Loving* (50th ed., p. 54). Harper Perennial - Modern Classics. (Original work published 1956)

Geis, G. (1978). Rape-in-marriage: law and law reform in England, the United States, and Sweden. *Digital.library.adelaide.edu.au, ALR Vol. 6, Noes 1-3, 1977-1978*(Adelaide Law Review, 1978; 6(2):284-303). https://digital.library.adelaide.edu.au/dspace/handle/2440/248

Glamour. (2019, March 17). *This clever new neuroscience-backed wellness trend will help you take charge of your body, brain, schedule, and life*. https://www.glamourmagazine.co.uk/article/physical-intelligence-claire-dale-and-patricia-peyton-extract

Holt, Dr. F. (2016, April 19). *Women in Greek Democracy – More Oppressed than Ever* (M. A. McIntosh, Ed.). https://brewminate.com/women-in-greek-democracy-more-oppressed-than-ever/

Indian Law Resource Center. (2021). *Ending Violence Against Native Women | Indian Law Resource Center*. Indianlaw.org. https://indianlaw.org/issue/ending-violence-against-native-women

Kroeger, C. C., & Nason-Clark, N. (2001). *No Place for Abuse-Biblical and Practical Resources to Counteract Domestic Violence* (p. 98). Inter-Varsity Press.

Kushner, H. S. (1981). *When Bad Things Happen to Good People*. Anchor Books, A Division of Random House.

Mayo Clinic Staff. (2020, October 27). *How to build resiliency*. https://www.mayoclinic.org/tests-procedures/resilience-training/in-depth/resilience/art-20046311#

Mulford, Ph.D., C., & Giordano, Ph.D., P. C. (2008, October 26). *Teen Dating Violence: A Closer Look at Adolescent Romantic Relationships*. National Institute of Justice. https://nij.ojp.gov/topics/articles/teen-dating-violence-closer-look-adolescent-romantic-relationships

National Center for Injury Prevention and Control, & Division of Violence Prevention. (2019). Preventing Teen Dating Violence. Center for Disease Control and Prevention. https://www.cdc.gov/violenceprevention/intimatepartnerviolence/teendatingviolence/fastfact.html

National Coalition Against Domestic Violence. (2021). *Statistics*. Ncadv.org. https://ncadv.org/statistics

National Institute of Justice. (2018, November 20). *Risk Factors in Pre- and Mid-Adolescence May Help Predict Dating Violence in Young Adulthood*. National Institute of Justice. https://nij.ojp.gov/topics/articles/risk-factors-pre-and-mid-adolescence-may-help-predict-dating-violence-young

National Network to End Domestic Violence. (2018, November 28). *16 Things You May Not Know About Domestic Violence*. NNEDV. https://nnedv.org/latest_update/16-things-may-not-know-domestic-violence/

Office on Women's Health, & US Department of Health and Human Services. (2017, October 10). *How to report abuse if you're an immigrant woman*. Womenshealth.gov. https://www.womenshealth.gov/relationships-and-safety/other-types/immigrant-and-refugee-women

One Love Foundation. (2020, April 20). *Statistics on Relationship Abuse*. https://www.joinonelove.org/statistics-on-relationship-abuse/

Oprah Winfrey. (2019). *The Path Made Clear: Discovering Your Life's Direction and Purpose* (pp. 22, 125,). Pan Macmillan.

Pahr, K. (2019, July 19). Perspective | Is teen sexting cause for concern, or no big deal? How to help kids stay safe online. https://www.washingtonpost.com/lifestyle/2019/07/19/is-teen-sexting-cause-concern-or-no-big-deal-how-help-kids-stay-safe-online/

Ruiz, M., & Mills, J.(1997). *The Four Agreements: A Practical Guide to Personal Freedom*. (Vol.31). Amber-Allen.

Schatz, C. (2009, August 21). *John Piper: "What should a wife's submission to her husband look like if he's an abuser?"* Women in Ministry. https://strivetoenter.com/wim/2009/08/21/john-piper-on-submission-in-abuse/

Suttle, T. (2011, September 13). *The Failure of the Megachurch.* https://www.huffpost.com/entry/the-failure-of-the-megachurch_b_954482

US Citizenship and Immigration Services. (2011, January 11). *Information on the Legal Rights Available to Immigrant Victims of Domestic Violence in the United States and Facts about Immigrating on a Marriage-Based Visa Fact Sheet | USCIS.* uscis.gov. https://www.uscis.gov/archive/information-on-the-legal-rights-available-to-immigrant-victims-of-domestic-violence-in-the-united

Van Beek, J. (2021). *SERMON: The Bent-Over Woman.* Sojourners. https://sojo.net/sites/default/files/downloads/the_bent-over_woman.pdf

Wagner, B. B. (2019, September 21). *The Shocking History of Virgin Tests and Cures.* https://www.ancient-origins.net/history-ancient-traditions/virginity-0012610

Weiss, E. (2000). *Surviving Domestic Violence: Voices of Women Who Broke Free* (1st ed.). Agreka Books.

Wigington, P. (2021, Winter 10). *Cult of Domesticity: Definition and History.* ThoughtCo. www.thoughtco.com/cult-of-domesticity-

Wilcox, A. (2019, January 23). Sexual Violence Rates Double Against Native American Women. The Daily Universe. https://universe.byu.edu/2019/01/23/sexual-violence-rates-higher-against-native-women-in-amerca-1/

Acknowledgements

If not for the encouragement of friends and family, their help with accountability, and their consistent love and support, this book would not be possible.

Special thanks and gratitude to my children-the five. You are and have always been my muse, my squad, my team, and my daily inspiration. Absolutely no one comes closer to my heart than you.

Thank you to my sister-friend Sheila Mathis. We met serving veterans and became great friends. Thank you for being a most excellent listener, coach, and leader by example. Your beautiful servant heart helped me bring this to fruition.

Thanks to my spiritual mother, Pastor Patricia, whom I met through Sheila. Your transparency, encouragement, and enthusiasm is such a blessing to me.

Thank you to my "Bestie" since ninth grade, Kenneth W. Andrews Jr., for all the talks late into the night, and allowing me to be me. I love you, your spirit, and your soul. I appreciate your constancy and the fact that you always have a song for everything.

Thank you to my friend and performing arts partner Ray Angelo Williams, aka "Hollywood." Your encouragement, openness, protection, and the ability to make me laugh at the world's insanity has been life to me. Thank you for the wisdom of "get it off of you" and your unique ability to pull the reigns when I go from zero to 1,000.

Thank you Sheila Selby. We just met and I appreciate your listening ear, humble spirit, and the wisdom you imparted to me during our drives together.

Thank you to so many others whose names are not mentioned that have aided and supported me in the ten plus years it took me to bring this work to fruition.

Other Published Works By K. J. Sharpe

Sistah, Can You Feel Me

Recalculating

Living with the Ancients
How History and Religion Impact Violence Against Women

Love Like Rain

CRAZY
(Stage Play)

The Bride
(Stage Play)

In the Beginning
(Children's Stage Play)

ABOUT THE AUTHOR

K. J. Sharpe is an award-winning writer, independent theatre director, choreographer, and producer, development specialist, and social change agent. She is a domestic violence overcomer who shares her life experiences to help people get through some of the toughest obstacles in their lives. Her goal has always been to educate, empower, inspire, and transform. Mother of five and grandmother of nine, she has worked as a volunteer with the Domestic Abuse Project of Delaware County, the Suicide Prevention Coalition, and other agencies aimed at helping women, children, youth, and veterans in crisis.

www.ingramcontent.com/pod-product-compliance
Lightning Source LLC
Chambersburg PA
CBHW052037090426
42739CB00010B/1940